Jonathan Edwards

Engraved by J. Dantz from a picture supposed to be by Copley in possession of Mrs Elizabeth Edwards Hartford Ct

(The frontispiece to Charles W. Elliott, *The New England History* [New York: Charles Scribner, 1857], vol. II)

"A Sweet Flame":

Piety in the Letters
of Jonathan Edwards

by
Michael A. G. Haykin

with a foreword by
George S. Claghorn

Reformation Heritage Books
Grand Rapids, Michigan

PROFILES IN REFORMED SPIRITUALITY

series editors—Joel R. Beeke and Michael A.G. Haykin

Books in the Series:

Michael Haykin, *"A Consuming Fire": The Piety of Alexander Whyte of Free St. George's*

Michael Haykin, *"A Sweet Flame": Piety in the Letters of Jonathan Edwards*

© 2007 by Michael A. G. Haykin

Published by
Reformation Heritage Books
2965 Leonard St., NE
Grand Rapids, MI 49525
616-977-0599 / Fax: 616-285-3246
e-mail: orders@heritagebooks.org
website: www.heritagebooks.org

ISBN 978-1-60178-011-9

Library of Congress Cataloging-in-Publication Data
Edwards, Jonathan, 1703-1758.
  "A sweet flame": piety in the letters of Jonathan Edwards / by
Michael A.G. Haykin.
      p. cm. — (Profiles in reformed spirituality)
  ISBN 978-1-60178-011-9 (pbk.: alk. paper)
  1. Edwards, Jonathan, 1703-1758—Correspondence.
  2. Congregational churches—New England—Clergy—
      Correspondence. I. Haykin, Michael A. G. II. Title.
BX7260.E3A4 2007
285.8092--dc22
  [B]
                          2007013188

To

Alison,
"my dear companion"

Table of Contents

Abbreviations

Letters and Personal Writings
Jonathan Edwards, *Letters and Personal Writings*, ed. George S. Claghorn, vol. 16 of *The Works of Jonathan Edwards* (New Haven/London: Yale University Press, 1998).

Marsden
George M. Marsden, *Jonathan Edwards: A Life* (New Haven/London: Yale University Press, 2003).

"Memoirs"
Sereno E. Dwight, "Memoirs of Jonathan Edwards, A. M." in *The Works of Jonathan Edwards*, revised and corr. Edward Hickman (1834 ed.; repr. Edinburgh: The Banner of Truth Trust, 1987), vol. 1.

Murray
Iain H. Murray, *Jonathan Edwards—A New Biography* (Edinburgh: The Banner of Truth Trust, 1987).

Profiles in Reformed Spirituality

Charles Dickens' famous line in *A Tale of Two Cities*—
"it was the best of times, it was the worst of times"
—seems well suited to western Evangelicalism since
the 1960s. On the one hand, these decades have seen
much for which to praise God and to rejoice. In His
goodness and grace, for instance, Reformed truth is
no longer a house under siege. Growing numbers
identify themselves theologically with what we hold
to be biblical truth, namely, Reformed theology and
piety. And yet, as an increasing number of Reformed
authors have noted, there are many sectors of the
surrounding western Evangelicalism that are charac-
terized by great shallowness and a trivialization of the
weighty things of God. So much of Evangelical worship seems barren. And when it comes to spirituality,
there is little evidence of the riches of our heritage as
Reformed Evangelicals.

As it was at the time of the Reformation, when the
watchword was *ad fontes*—"back to the sources"—so
it is now: the way forward is backward. We need to
go back to the spiritual heritage of Reformed Evangelicalism to find the pathway forward. We cannot
live in the past; to attempt to do so would be anti-
quarianism. But our Reformed forebearers in the faith

can teach us much about Christianity, its doctrines, its passions, and its fruit.

And they can serve as our role models. As R. C. Sproul has noted of such giants as Augustine, Martin Luther, John Calvin, and Jonathan Edwards: "These men all were conquered, overwhelmed, and spiritually intoxicated by their vision of the holiness of God. Their minds and imaginations were captured by the majesty of God the Father. Each of them possessed a profound affection for the sweetness and excellence of Christ. There was in each of them a singular and unswerving loyalty to Christ that spoke of a citizenship in heaven that was always more precious to them than the applause of men."[1]

To be sure, we would not dream of placing these men and their writings alongside the Word of God. John Jewel (1522-1571), the Anglican apologist, once stated: "What say we of the fathers, Augustine, Ambrose, Jerome, Cyprian?... They were learned men, and learned fathers; the instruments of the mercy of God, and vessels full of grace. We despise them not, we read them, we reverence them, and give thanks unto God for them. Yet...we may not make them the foundation and warrant of our conscience: we may not put our trust in them. Our trust is in the name of the Lord."[2]

Seeking then both to honor the past and yet not idolize it, we are issuing these books in the series

1. "An Invaluable Heritage," *Tabletalk*, 23, no. 10 (October 1999): 5-6.

2. Cited in Barrington R. White, "Why Bother with History?" *Baptist History and Heritage*, 4, no. 2 (July 1969): 85.

Profiles in Reformed Spirituality. The design is to introduce the spirituality and piety of the Reformed tradition by presenting descriptions of the lives of notable Christians with select passages from their works. This combination of biographical sketches and collected portions from primary sources gives a taste of the subjects' contributions to our spiritual heritage and some direction as to how the reader can find further edification through their works. It is the hope of the publishers that this series will provide riches for those areas where we are poor and light of day where we are stumbling in the deepening twilight.

—Joel R. Beeke
Michael A. G. Haykin

Foreword

━━━━•⊶•⊷•━━━━

A rare privilege awaits you. In these pages, you are about to meet one of the great Christians of all time: Jonathan Edwards!

Your guide is reliable. Dr. Haykin has gathered some of the choicest letters of Edwards. In them, you will discover the insights of this noble leader on "Piety," up close and personal. Piety? That is the way we tap the resources God provides, to live for His glory and help others find them, too.

Before going on to the high ridges of thought, your escort will sketch the chief events of Edwards' life. Then, in the letters, you will find Edwards' views on piety, in his own words.

Treasures for all ages are here. Edwards tells how he found heaven within, God's mighty presence, enabling him to meet every challenge and be more than conqueror. Best of all, he had the radiant hope of being at home with the Lord in the life beyond.

Bringing the eternal into practical situations is no mean feat. Edwards, however, accomplishes just that. We see his role as a child, husband, parent, pastor, mentor, and educator—with pungent thoughts on conversion, prayer, the Bible, revival, evangelism, and other vital topics. Each fruit of the Spirit is to be found here, expressed in Edwards' own words, demonstrated in his life.

The selections were chosen wisely. We are all indebted to Dr. Haykin for his outstanding service in making these classics available in such an attractive format.

Now, to savor them!

George S. Claghorn
Lansdale, Pennsylvania

Acknowledgements

This small selection of Jonathan Edwards' letters is deeply indebted to the definitive collection made by George Claghorn in what is now Volume 16 of the Yale University Press edition of *The Works of Jonathan Edwards, Letters and Personal Writings* (1998). Prior to Claghorn's edition—over thirty-five years in the making[1]—there were a few selections of Edwards' works that contained some of his letters,[2] but nothing substantial. With Claghorn's superb edition, the student of Edwards can now see something of the range of Edwards' correspondence, from influential Boston ministers like Benjamin Colman to the leading evange-

1. See George S. Claghorn, "Transcribing a Difficult Hand: Collecting and Editing Edwards' Letters over Thirty-Five Years" in D.G. Hart, Sean Michael Lucas and Stephen J. Nichols, eds., *The Legacy of Jonathan Edwards: American Religion and the Evangelical Tradition* (Grand Rapids: Baker, 2003), 217-227.

2. See, for example, Vergilius Ferm, *Puritan Sage: Collected Writings of Jonathan Edwards* (New York: Library Publishers, 1953), 617-620, 637-640; Clarence H. Faust and Thomas H. Johnson, *Jonathan Edwards: Representative Selections* (rev. ed.; New York: Hill and Wang, 1962), 382-415; John E. Smith, Harry S. Stout, and Kenneth P. Minkema, eds., *A Jonathan Edwards Reader* (New Haven/London: Yale University Press, 1995), 298-325. See also Bernard Bangley, ed. and modernized, *Awakening: The Essential Writings of Jonathan Edwards* (Brewster, Massachusetts: Paraclete Press, 2004), 154-164.

list of Edwards' era, namely George Whitefield, from important colonial figures like Sir William Pepperrell to notable Scottish preachers such as John Erskine.[3] Edwards also wrote, though, to lesser-known individuals whose names do not normally appear in historical studies of Edwards and his era, from young believers like Deborah Hatheway[4] to Boston booksellers.[5] This volume, then, fills a lacuna by giving those interested in the life and work of Edwards a book-length selection of his correspondence. However, this selection does have a focus: Edwardsean piety. An attempt has been made to provide a number of vistas by which this area of Edwards' life—so central to all of his theological and intellectual pursuits—can be viewed, and, it is hoped, be a challenge to Christian faith and practice in our day.

In a review of George Marsden's biography of Edwards—*Jonathan Edwards: A Life* (2003)—Ted Rivera has noted that while Edwards' thinking about various issues of theology, such as original sin, are accessible, "it is almost impossible to peer into his inmost private thoughts" in his latter years. As proof, he cites the fact that while there are three thousand of Martin Luther's letters extant, Claghorn's herculean efforts came up with only 236 of Edwards' letters.[6] This is quite remarkable and indeed lamentable, but

---

3. Claghorn, "Transcribing a Difficult Hand," 224.

4. See below, pages 41-47.

5. See Jonathan Edwards, Letters to Jacob Wendell, August 8, 1737 and August 23, 1737 (*Letters and Personal Writings*, 70-71).

6. "*Jonathan Edwards: A Life*, by George M. Marsden," *Faith & Mission*, 23, no. 2 (Spring 2006): 121.

in the letters that survive we do get rich glimpses of the passions that stirred Edwards' soul to the depths: books and biblical reflection, revival and the salvation of sinners, prayer and the spread of the gospel to the ends of the earth, his family and the spiritual health of his wife and children—and above all, Christ and His glory. Hopefully, there is enough here in this small volume that will spur the reader on to delight in the God whom Edwards loved—and still does love.

I am deeply grateful to Steve and Lois Krogh for their hospitality in Jenison, Michigan, while I was finishing the initial draft of this book, and for their friendship. I also want to thank Jay T. Collier of Reformation Heritage Books, who has overseen this project and guided it into print, and for the team that works under his direction: Sharla Kattenberg (copy editing), Linda den Hollander (typesetting), and Amy Zevenbergen (cover design). Thanks are due Hélène Grondines for the painting of Edwards that adorns the front cover. Additionally I am indebted in various ways to Pastor Ron Baines (for photographs taken), to Pastors Scott Bowman and Steve Raemisch (for encouraging words and deeds), and Janice van Eck (for scanning most of the illustrations). I also want to thank George Claghorn for writing the foreword.

In the editing of these letters, most of them drawn from Sereno E. Dwight's biography of his great-grandfather, capitalization, punctuation and spelling have been uniformly modernized, and Edwards' long Latinate paragraphs broken down into smaller, manageable units. Various notes have been added to provide the reader with the historical background to these letters and to give some information about those to whom they were addressed. Often these notes point out further articles and books where the reader can find out more about the context and original recipients of the letters. For indispensable help in transcribing these letters I wish to thank Christina Case.

As a note of interest, the emblem used to end most of the selections is taken from a stone frieze on the Edwards Church of Northampton, Massachusetts.

When Edwards was recommending the first major work by his friend and confidant Joseph Bellamy to his Scottish correspondent John Erskine, namely Bellamy's *True Religion Delineated* (1750), the New England divine told Erskine: "I am fully satisfied that his aim in this publication is not his own fame and reputation in the world; but the glory of God, and the advancement of the kingdom of his Redeemer."[7] What a noble goal to aspire to for any Christian author—or editor!

Dundas, Ontario
March 17, 2007

---

7. Letter to John Erskine, July 5, 1750 ("Memoirs," cxviii). See below, page 118.

President Edwards was one of the greatest, best, and most useful men of this age.... And there is reason to hope, that though dead, he will yet speak for ages to come, to the great advantage of the church of Christ, and the immortal welfare of many souls—and that his publications will produce a yet greater harvest of happiness to man and glory to God in the day of the Lord.

—Samuel Hopkins (1721-1803)

Jonathan Edwards

(A portrait by Hélène Grondines, 2006)

The Piety of Jonathan Edwards
(1703-1758)

Jonathan Edwards (1703-1758) has been rightly described as "the greatest Christian theologian of the eighteenth century."[1] At the beginning of his life, the Reformed faith was increasingly a house under siege in the transatlantic world as the Enlightenment, with its stress on the omnicompetence of human reason, was apparently relegating to the dustbin of history every worldview that asserted the priority of revelation. The Edwardsean corpus, composed of various occasional pieces and robust systematic treatises like *A careful and strict Enquiry into The modern prevailing Notions of...Freedom of Will* (1754), was key to the overall Christian rebuttal of the *mentalité* of the Enlightenment and the restoration of Calvinism to a place of spiritual vigor and influence.

In the realm of spiritual theology and Evangelical piety, Edwards' writings—especially those on revival—also exercised a remarkable influence. Edwards was deeply indebted to the passionate interest that seventeenth-century Puritanism had in the

---

1. Miklós Vetö, "Book Reviews: *America's Theologian: A Recommendation of Jonathan Edwards.* By Robert W. Jenson," *Church History*, 58 (1989): 522.

work of the Holy Spirit.[2] Along with being an heir
to this profound pneumatological interest, Edwards
found himself called upon to respond to both tren-
chant criticism of the Great Awakening (1740-1742),
in which he played a central role, and clear fanaticism on the part of certain supporters of the revival.
The result was some of the richest literature in the
history of the church on the nature of genuine Christian piety.[3]

Early Years

What is remarkable, though, about this theological
achievement is that Edwards lived most of his life on
the edge of the transatlantic British Empire, far from
the centers of literary power and influence in that
world. Born on October 5, 1703, at East Windsor,
Connecticut, his father, Timothy Edwards (d. 1758),
was the pastor of the town's Congregational Church.[4]
His mother, Esther, was the daughter of Solomon
Stoddard (1643-1729), the enormously influential
pastor of the Congregationalist Church in Northampton, Massachusetts, due north of East Windsor.

---

2. For example, for a clear link between the piety of Edwards' *Life
of David Brainerd* (1748) and that of the New England Puritan Thomas
Shepard (1605-1649), see Charles E. Hambrick-Stowe, "The Spirit of
the Old Writers: The Great Awakening and the Persistence of Puritan
Piety" in Francis J. Bremer, ed., *Puritanism: Transatlantic Perspectives
on a Seventeenth-Century Anglo-American Faith* (Boston: Massachusetts
Historical Society, 1993), 288-289.

3. See Michael A.G. Haykin, *Jonathan Edwards: The Holy Spirit in
Revival* (Darlington, Co. Durham: Evangelical Press, 2005).

4. Especially helpful for understanding Edwards' life are Murray and Marsden. See now also Philip F. Gura, *Jonathan Edwards:
America's Evangelical* (New York: Hill and Wang, 2005).

Edwards was the fifth of his parents' eleven children—ten girls and Jonathan! Edwards' sisters grew to be tall women and those who knew them often spoke of Timothy Edwards' "sixty feet of daughters."[5] Remarkable for that day, Timothy Edwards encouraged them to develop both intellectually and spiritually.[6] In fact, in his early childhood, Jonathan was tutored not only by his Puritan father but also by his older sisters.[7]

Iain Murray, in his biography of Edwards, reckons that the preponderance of females in Edwards' early years helped shape the "gentleness of Jonathan's bearing in later life."[8] Actually, the Edwards sisters were strong, often single-minded women, who were not afraid to speak their minds. For instance, during the Great Awakening (1740-1742), Edwards' eldest sister, Esther (1695-1766), was firmly opposed to the revival. In a diary entry for August 1743 she noted, "I was last night in company with one of the 'New Lights.' I could hardly bear the room." Nor did she keep her views to herself and enclosed in her diary. The following March, she made known her problems with the revival to her brother, and they had a strong disagreement about the awakening. In her diary, she wrote, "Some things occurred this morning which made it appear very doubtful whether my dear

---

5. Murray, 9.

6. On Jonathan's sisters, see Kenneth P. Minkema, "Hannah and Her Sisters: Sisterhood, Courtship, and Marriage in the Edwards Family in the Early Eighteenth Century," *The New England Historical and Genealogical Register* (January 1992): 35-56.

7. Minkema, "Hannah and Her Sisters," 41.

8. Murray, 9.

brother would ever come off of some principles which appeared to me were detrimental to religion."[9]

On the other hand, his sisters were also women of great piety. Before her early death, Jerusha (1710-1729), one of Jonathan's younger sisters, was known for her "solitary meditations, contemplative walks in the woods, and late-night Scripture readings."[10]

A Word-shaped Spirituality

In 1716 Edwards entered the Collegiate School of Connecticut in New Haven (later to become Yale University), graduating from there in 1720 with a B.A. Subsequent studies led to an M.A. in 1723. Between these two degrees, he underwent conversion, which probably took place in the spring of 1721.[11] As he was reading 1 Timothy 1:17,[12] Edwards later said that

> there came into my soul, and was as it were diffused through it, a sense of the glory of the Divine Being; a new sense, quite different from any thing I ever experienced before. Never any words of scripture seemed to me as these words did. I thought with myself, how excellent a Being that was; and how happy I should be, if I might enjoy that God, and be rapt up to him in Heaven, and be as it were swallowed up in him for ever.... From about that time, I began to have a new kind of apprehensions and ideas of Christ, and the work of redemption, and the glorious way of salvation

---

9. Minkema, "Hannah and Her Sisters," 42.

10. Minkema, "Hannah and Her Sisters," 38.

11. For the date of Edwards' conversion, see Murray, 35.

12. "Now unto the king eternal, immortal, invisible, the only wise God, be honour and glory for ever and ever, Amen."

by him. An inward, sweet sense of these things, at times, came into my heart; and my soul was led away in pleasant views and contemplations of them. And my mind was greatly engaged to spend my time in reading and meditating on Christ, on the beauty and excellency of his person, and the lovely way of salvation, by free grace in him.[13]

It is vital, first of all, to note that Scripture was central to his conversion. Not surprisingly, he would later maintain that Scripture needs to be central in all preaching and Christian piety, for the Scriptures "are the light by which ministers must be enlightened, and the light they are to hold forth to their hearers; and they are the fire whence their hearts and the hearts of their hearers must be enkindled."[14] In an unpublished sermon on 1 Corinthians 2:11-13—preached in 1740—Edwards can thus emphasize:

Ministers ought not to preach those things which their own wisdom and reason suggest, but the things that are already dictated by the Spirit of God.... Their preaching ought to rely on what [is] revealed and discovered to their minds by an understanding infinitely superior to others.[15]

In the above text about his conversion Edwards also highlights the "inward, sweet sense" that gripped

---

13. *Personal Narrative* (*Letters and Personal Writings*, 792-793).

14. *The True Excellency of a Gospel Minister* (*The Works of Jonathan Edwards*, revised and corr. Edward Hickman [1834 ed.; repr. Edinburgh/Carlisle, Pennsylvania: Banner of Truth Trust, 1974], 2:959).

15. Cited in Helen Petter Westra, "'Above All Others': Jonathan Edwards and the Gospel Ministry," *American Presbyterians: Journal of Presbyterian History*, 67, no. 3 (Fall 1989): 212.

his soul as he meditated upon what Scripture says about God and Christ and their utterly free and sovereign grace in salvation. Such biblical meditation would become central to his piety. Samuel Hopkins (1721-1803), one of his close friends and his first biographer, noted that Edwards was, "as far as it can be known, much on his knees in secret, and in devout reading of God's word and meditation upon it."[16] Advice he gave his daughter, Mary, thus came very much out of his own walk with God: "Retire often from this vain world, from all its bubbles and empty shadows, and vain amusements, and converse with God alone."[17]

Speaking around 1740 of his encounter with Scripture in the months immediately after his conversion, Edwards noted:

> I had then, and at other times, the greatest delight in the holy Scriptures, of any book whatsoever. Oftentimes in reading it, every word seemed to touch my heart. I felt an harmony between something in my heart, and those sweet and powerful words. I seemed often to see so much light, exhibited by every sentence, and such a refreshing ravishing food communicated, that I could not get along in reading. Used oftentimes to dwell long on one sentence, to see the wonders contained [in] it; and yet almost every sentence seemed to be full of wonders.[18]

---

16. "The Life and Character of the Late Reverend Mr. Jonathan Edwards" in David Levin, ed., *Jonathan Edwards: A Profile* (New York: Hill and Wang, 1969), 39.

17. See below, pages 108-109.

18. *Personal Narrative* (*Letters and Personal Writings*, 797).

This pattern of meditation upon God's Holy
Word, one that was part of Edwards' Puritan heritage, appears to have been central to Edwards' walk
with God in the latter years of his life as well. Samuel
Hopkins noted that Edwards "had an uncommon
thirst for knowledge, in the pursuit of which, he
spared no cost nor pains." He thus "read all the
books, especially books of divinity," that he could
get hold of. This passion for and delight in books is
very evident in a number of the letters reproduced
below.[19] But, Hopkins emphasized, "he studied the
Bible more than all other books, and more than most
other divines do. His uncommon acquaintance with
the Bible appears in his sermons, and in most of his
publications; and his great pains in studying it are
manifest in his manuscript notes upon it."[20]

For Edwards, the Scriptures were "the great and
standing rule for the direction of his [i.e. God's]
church in all religious matters, and concerns of their
souls in all ages."[21] Thus, for example, he was a convinced Calvinist not primarily because of the teaching
of John Calvin, but because he believed Calvinism
was first and foremost scriptural truth.[22] "I utterly
disclaim," he wrote in the Preface to *A careful and strict
Enquiry into The modern prevailing Notions of…Freedom*

19. See below, pages 83-86, 95-97, 103, 113-118, 141-143.

20. Cited "Life and Character of the Late Reverend Mr. Jonathan
Edwards" in Levin, ed., *Jonathan Edwards*, 40-41.

21. *The Distinguishing Marks of a Work of the Spirit of God* (C.C.
Goen, ed., *Jonathan Edwards: The Great Awakening*, vol. 4 of *The Works
of Jonathan Edwards* [New Haven: Yale University Press, 1972], 253).

22. Hopkins, "Life and Character of the Late Reverend Mr. Jonathan Edwards" in Levin, ed., *Jonathan Edwards*, 52.

of Will (1754), "a dependence on Calvin, or believing the doctrines which I hold, because he believed and taught them."[23]

A further example of the fruit of his life-long meditation on Scripture can be seen in what has been termed Edwards' "Blank Bible." This was a small printed Bible that Edwards owned in which blank sheets were placed between all of the pages. These blank sheets were divided into two columns so that Edwards could then write commentary on adjacent texts. Edwards' "Blank Bible" contains as many as 10,000 entries, written on the entire Bible between 1730 and 1758.[24]

It is this profound Bible knowledge, for instance, that underlies the rich pastoral wisdom displayed in the letter to his first cousin, Elnathan Whitman (1709-1772), and that to his friend Mary Pepperrell.[25]

Family Piety

In 1726, Edwards was invited to become the assistant pastor to his grandfather, Solomon Stoddard. When Stoddard died in 1729, Edwards became the sole pastor of the church. Now, within a year of his coming to Northampton, he had married. He had met his bride, Sarah Pierpont (1710-1758), first when she was 13. Like Jonathan, Sarah was born into a family

---

23. *Freedom of the Will*, ed. Paul Ramsey (*The Works of Jonathan Edwards*, vol. 1 [New Haven: Yale University Press, 1957]), 131.

24. Stephen J. Stein, "The Spirit and the Word: Jonathan Edwards and Scriptural Exegesis" in Nathan O. Hatch and Harry S. Stout, eds., *Jonathan Edwards and the American Experience* (New York/ Oxford: Oxford University Press, 1988), 121.

25. See below, pages 67-75, 123-131.

rich in spiritual privilege. Her father, James Pierpont
(d. 1714), was a Congregationalist minister and one
of the founders of Yale College, while her mother,
née Mary Hooker, was the grand-daughter of Thomas
Hooker (1586-1647), one of the founders of Puritan
New England.

Jonathan's first recorded words about his future
wife are well known. Writing in 1723, he said of her:

> They say there is a young lady in [New Haven]
> who is beloved of that almighty Being, who made
> and rules the world, and that there are certain
> seasons in which this Great Being, in some way
> or other invisible, comes to her and fills her
> mind with exceeding sweet delight, and that she
> hardly cares for any thing, except to meditate on
> him—that she expects after a while to be received
> up where he is, to be raised out of the world and
> caught up into heaven; being assured that he loves
> her too well to let her remain at a distance from
> him always. There she is to dwell with him, and
> to be ravished with his love, favor and delight for-
> ever. Therefore, if you present all the world before
> her, with the richest of its treasures, she disregards
> it and cares not for it, and is unmindful of any pain
> or affliction. She has a strange sweetness in her
> mind, and sweetness of temper, uncommon purity
> in her affections; is most just and praiseworthy in
> all her actions; and you could not persuade her to
> do anything thought wrong or sinful, if you would
> give her all the world, lest she should offend this
> great Being. She is of a wonderful sweetness, calm-
> ness and universal benevolence of mind; especially
> after those times in which this great God has mani-
> fested himself to her mind. She will sometimes go

about, singing sweetly, from place to [place]; and
she seems to be always full of joy and pleasure;
and no one knows for what. She loves to be alone,
and to wander in the fields and on the mountains,
and seems to have someone invisible always con-
versing with her.[26]

Though Sarah was but thirteen when Edwards
wrote this, what he called Sarah's "wonderful
sweetness" was deeply impressive. Her sweetness
of mind and temper, her sweet singing, and the
"exceeding sweet delight" that she had in God especially appealed to Edwards, for whom the adjective
"sweet" and its derivatives was frequently on his lips
when he spoke of God and divine things.[27] By God's
grace Edwards had found a soul-mate: her affective
piety and commitment to meditation upon God and
spiritual things were in perfect harmony with his
spirituality of the Word. Four years later Jonathan
and Sarah were married.

"The man whose heart is endeared to the woman
he loves," wrote Sarah's great-grandfather Thomas
Hooker, "he dreams of her in the night, hath her in
his eye and apprehension when he awakes, museth
on her as he sits at table."[28] Though not at all the
sort of remark that the contemporary world associ-

---

26. *Letters and Personal Writings*, 789-790.

27. Leonard I. Sweet notes that the word "sweet" was "incontest-
ably Edwards's favorite word" ("The Laughter of One: Sweetness
and Light in Franklin and Edwards" in Barbara B. Oberg and Harry
S. Stout, eds., *Benjamin Franklin, Jonathan Edwards, and the Representation of American Culture* [New York/Oxford: Oxford University Press,
1993], 126).

28. Cited Elisabeth D. Dodds, *Marriage to a Difficult Man: The*

ates with the Puritans, it is actually a typical Puritan sentiment, for the Puritans reveled in the joys of marriage. And in this regard, Jonathan Edwards is one with his Puritan forebears. This is not the way that the contemporary world remembers Edwards, who so often today is depicted as sour-spirited and ill-tempered, "dark and gloomy," a "most bitter hater of man."[29] How different was the real Edwards and how sparkling with life, piety, and beauty his family and home!

From his parents Edwards learned the vital importance of conjugal love to a marriage. In a sermon that he preached on June 28, 1730, Timothy Edwards had stressed that a man's love for his wife must be "a singular, peculiar thing," in which he was never to abuse his authority as head of the home but to act "in a loving manner with due respect to his wife."[30] The influence of his parents' marriage upon Jonathan can be clearly seen when one reads in the early biography of Edwards written by Samuel Hopkins, who had lived in the Edwards household, that Edwards "maintained a great esteem and regard for his amiable and excellent consort. Much of the tender and kind was expressed in his conversation with her and conduct towards her."[31] And it is seen especially in his

---

"Uncommon Union" of Jonathan and Sarah Edwards (Philadelphia: Westminster Press, 1971), 18.

29. For these descriptions, see Sweet, "Laughter of One" in Oberg and Stout, eds., *Benjamin Franklin, Jonathan Edwards, and the Representation of American Culture*, 116-117.

30. Cited Minkema, "Hannah and Her Sisters," 37.

31. "Life and Character of the Late Reverend Mr. Jonathan Edwards" in Levin, ed., *Jonathan Edwards*, 42-43.

final words for his wife who was not present when he died—"Give my kindest love to my dear wife, and tell her that the uncommon union, which has so long subsisted between us has been of such a nature, as I trust is spiritual, and therefore will continue forever."[32]

Sarah and Jonathan had eleven children, all of whom survived infancy. Hopkins clearly states that his children "reverenced, esteemed, and loved him."[33] His third daughter, Esther Burr (1732-1758), for example, in a fascinating diary that she kept from 1754 to 1757, has this revealing entry for September 19, 1756:

> Last eve I had some free discourse with my Father on the great things that concern my best intrest—I opend my difficulties to him very freely and he as freely advised and directed. The conversation has removed some distressing doubts that discouraged me much in my Christian warfare—He gave me some excellent directions to be observed in secret that tend to keep the soul near to God, as well as others to be observed in a more publick way—What a mercy that I have such a Father! Such a Guide![34]

Jonathan's role as spiritual mentor to his children had begun when each of them was very small. Hopkins observed that Jonathan "took opportuni-

---

32. See below, page 155.

33. "Life and Character of the Late Reverend Mr. Jonathan Edwards" in Levin, ed., *Jonathan Edwards*, 43.

34. *The Journal of Esther Edwards Burr, 1754-1757*, eds. Carol F. Karlsen and Laurie Crumpacker (New Haven/London: Yale University Press, 1984), 224.

ties to converse with them in his study, singly and
particularly about their own soul's concerns; and to
give them warning, exhortation, and direction, as he
saw occasion."[35] In addition to this, Edwards sought
to begin each day with family prayer, in which he
would read a chapter of God's Word—often, Hopkins recalls, this reading was done by candlelight in
the winter as they rose before sunrise—and ask his
children questions appropriate to their ages about the
text.[36] Once a week, each Saturday night, Jonathan
instructed his children in the *Westminster Shorter Cat-
echism*, "not merely by taking care that they learned
it by heart," Hopkins observes, "but by leading
them into an understanding of the doctrines therein
taught, by asking them questions on each answer, and
explaining it to them."[37]

We see something of this habitual concern for the
spiritual welfare of his children in some of his letters to them and remarks about them. Consider his
relationship to the four eldest, all daughters.[38] His
first daughter, Sarah (1728-1805), was born the year
following their marriage. Sarah tended to be sickly as
a child. On one occasion, when she was staying with
relatives in Lebanon, Connecticut, in the summer of
1741, Jonathan told her plainly in a letter that she had

---

35. "Life and Character of the Late Reverend Mr. Jonathan
Edwards" in Levin, ed., *Jonathan Edwards*, 43.

36. "Life and Character of the Late Reverend Mr. Jonathan
Edwards" in Levin, ed., *Jonathan Edwards*, 43.

37. "Life and Character of the Late Reverend Mr. Jonathan
Edwards" in Levin, ed., *Jonathan Edwards*, 43.

38. For a letter to his eldest son, Timothy, see below, pages
137-140.

"a very weak and infirm body" and as such she might not live long. If she, therefore, lived for the comforts of this world, she was apt to be disappointed, but, he went on,

> if your soul prospers you will be an happy blessed person, whatever becomes of your body. I wish you much of the presence of Christ and communion with him, and that you might live so as to give him honor in the place where you are by an amiable behavior towards all.[39]

As it happened, Sarah lived to seventy-six. But while her father misjudged Sarah's physical hardiness, his advice about and prayer for her spiritual health reveal a proper understanding of his calling as Sarah's father.

Following Sarah came Jerusha (1730-1748), deemed by her father before her death "as a very eminent saint" and one whom he described a few months after her death as "the flower of the family."[40] She died after nursing the dying David Brainerd (1718-1747). Her father had her buried right beside Brainerd in the Northampton cemetery, where today their bodies still lie awaiting the resurrection. After her death, Edwards drew great comfort from remembering what he called the "remarkable appearances of piety in her, from her childhood, in life, and also at her death."[41]

Esther (1732-1758) came next.[42] She married Aaron Burr, Sr. (1715-1757), the second president of the Col-

---

39. See below, page 49.

40. See below, page 98.

41. See below, page 99.

42. Esther's childhood years had coincided with the years of the

lege of New Jersey (later Princeton University). She, like Jerusha, displayed an ardent piety and infectious love for Christ. Her piety is well revealed by a diary that actually forms a series of letters to a close Boston friend, Sarah Prince (1728-1771)—the daughter of

---

Great Awakening. She was eight when the Great Awakening began and ten when it ended in 1742. All of this would have made a deep impression on her. Dwight ("Memoirs," clxxix) notes that Esther "appeared to be the subject of divine impressions, when seven or eight years old." The revival would no doubt have reinforced in her mind that genuine Christianity was a religion of the heart and that "the only true religion was indeed heartfelt, nothing short of a total and joyous submission to the will of God" (cited Karlsen and Crumpacker, eds., *Journal of Esther Edwards Burr*, 9). She herself made a profession of faith when she was "about fifteen" (Dwight, "Memoirs," clxxix).

On June 29, 1752, at the age of twenty, Esther married Aaron Burr, Sr. They had two children, a girl named Sarah and the boy, Aaron Burr, Jr. (1756-1836). The younger Burr later became the Vice-President of the United States. He is most remembered not for his term as Vice-President but for his killing of his political rival Alexander Hamilton in a duel in 1804. When the younger Burr died in 1836 after a lifetime without God, he was virtually friendless. Among his dying requests was that he be buried at the *feet* of his father and grandfather in Princeton, since he believed himself to be unworthy to be buried at their sides.

For her diary, see Karlsen and Crumpacker, eds., *Journal of Esther Edwards Burr*. For a brief biographical sketch of Esther, see Gerald R. McDermott, "Burr, Esther Edwards" in Donald M. Lewis, *The Blackwell Dictionary of Evangelical Biography 1730-1860* (Oxford/Cambridge, Massachusetts: Blackwell, 1995), I, 175. See also Lucia Bergamasco, "Amitié, amour et spiritualité dans la Nouvelle-Angleterre du XVIIe siècle: l'expérience d'Esther Burr et de Sarah Prince," *Annales ESC*, 41 (1986): 295-323 and the helpful chapter, "Through Esther's Eyes" in Murray, 399-420 and the various references in Marsden, *passim*. On Esther's Edwardsean piety, see Michael A.G. Haykin, *Jonathan Edwards: The Holy Spirit in Revival* (Darlington, Co. Durham: Evangelical Press, 2005), 171-177.

Thomas Prince (1687-1758)

Thomas Prince (1687-1758), pastor of Boston's Old South Church and a close friend of Edwards.[43]

For example, here she is speaking on the importance of Christian friends: "Nothing is more refreshing to the soul (except communication with God himself), than the company and society of a friend."[44] For the Christian, true friends are those with whom one can share the deepest things of one's life. Esther obviously views it as a means of grace, one of the ways that God the Holy Spirit keeps Christians in fellowship with the Savior.

The fourth Edwards daughter, Mary (1734-1807), married a judge by the name of Timothy Dwight (1726-1777) and lived to be an evangelical "matriarch."[45] One letter to her from her father survives. Edwards wrote it in the midst of the communion controversy that wracked the Northampton church between 1748 and 1750, and that ultimately led to Edwards' dismissal as pastor on June 22, 1750. But as George Claghorn rightly notes: "No matter how pressing the demands or cares of the moment,

---

43. Thomas Prince (1687-1758) was one of Edwards' close ministerial friends in Boston. He was the pastor of Boston's Old South Church. Marsden notes that Prince was the most learned of the Congregationalist ministers in Boston, "an expert in scientific matters" and one who was sometimes compared with Cotton Mather because of his wide learning (Marsden, 279). He was an ardent bibliophile. Much of the magnificent library he left at his death is now housed in the Boston Public Library.

44. *Journal of Esther Edwards Burr*, eds. Karlsen and Crumpacker, 185.

45. The description is that of Marsden, 355.

Edwards always put his paternal and pastoral respon-
sibilities first."[46]

Edwards begins the letter by expressing his concern for Mary's physical well-being, since she was
a considerable distance away, in Portsmouth, New
Hampshire. Yes, he stressed—and now he includes
Sarah as a co-writer of the letter:

> Though you are at so great a distance from us,
> yet God is everywhere. You are much out of the
> reach of our care, but you are every moment in his
> hands. We have not the comfort of seeing you, but
> he sees you. His eye is always upon you. And if
> you may but be sensibly nigh to him, and have his
> gracious presence, 'tis no matter though you are
> far distant from us. I had rather you should remain
> hundreds of miles distant from us and have God
> nigh to you by his Spirit, than to have you always
> with us, and live at a distance from God.[47]

There is little doubt that Jonathan and Sarah
delighted in having their children around them—
Edwards mentions here "the comfort" of their seeing
their daughter. But parental love must be kept in
its place. Far more important, was that God was
close to Mary by his Spirit. If that were so—if Mary,
in other words, were indwelt by the Spirit of God
because she had been converted—then Jonathan and
Sarah would be content to have Mary live "hundreds
of miles" away.

---

46. *Letters and Personal Writings*, 288. For a comment on this letter,
see also Marsden, 355.

47. See below, page 107.

Edwards thus went on to say his "daily prayer" for Mary was that she would meet with God where she was, "have much of his divine influences" on her heart, and in God's time come back to her earthly family, prospering in her soul. Never one to omit practical admonition, Edwards finished by giving his fourth daughter, who would have been fifteen at the time, some nuggets of Puritan-like advice.

> I hope that you will maintain a strict and constant watch over yourself and against all temptations: that you don't forget and forsake God; and particularly that you don't grow slack in secret religion. Retire often from this vain world, and all its bubbles, empty shadows, and vain amusements, and converse with God alone; and seek that divine grace and comfort, the least drop of which is worth more than all the riches, gaiety, pleasures and entertainments of the whole world.[48]

Edwards surely has in mind here the way that the world and all of its allurements seem so attractive to the young. The solution is times of solitude and prayer, when the worth of eternal realities may be rightly seen.

It should be noted that Mary's son, also named Timothy Dwight (1752-1817), became an illustrious President of Yale University and a key figure in the Second Great Awakening that began in the early 1790s and lasted well into the 1830s. Something of a child prodigy—he is said to have learned the alphabet in a day, was reading parts of the Bible at four and taking lessons in Latin by the age of six—Dwight

---

48. See below, pages 108-109.

Grave of Sarah Edwards at Princeton—
she was buried in the same grave as her husband.

made what has become a famous remark often attributed to others: "All that I am and all that I shall be, I owe to my mother."[49]

The "holy looseness" with which Jonathan and Sarah held Mary is true of their relationship with all of their children. When Edwards was ministering at Stockbridge, for example, he encouraged his son, the future theologian-pastor Jonathan Edwards, Jr. (1745-1801), to spend time learning the culture and language of the Oneida. The boy went with a missionary, Gideon Hawley, to an Oneida village at the head of the Susquehanna, about two hundred miles away from his family. The young boy was here from April 1755 to mid-January 1756. What amazing confidence the senior Edwards and his wife Sarah had in a sovereign God to send their son into such a potentially dangerous place!

In the winter of 1756, the situation did indeed become too dangerous for the young Jonathan and Gideon to stay with the Oneida. They trekked back to Fort Johnson, the fortified mansion of Sir William Johnson (1715-1774), now in present-day Amsterdam, New York. Johnson was a remarkable Irishman, born and raised not far from Dublin, who had come to America at the age of twenty-two. An extremely tall man, gargantuan in his day, Johnson was a resourceful businessman and went on to create a mini-empire in the Mohawk Valley. Key to this empire were his own brains and his third wife, a Mohawk by the name of Molly Brant (*c.* 1736-1796), or Koñwatsi'tsiaiéñni as she liked to be known. Her younger brother was

---

49. Dodds, *Marriage to a Difficult Man*, 209.

Joseph Brant (1742/43-1807), well-known in Canadian history. But Molly was actually much more powerful in her day, because Mohawk society was matriarchal and she was the wife of the one of the most powerful British land barons in that area of the New World.

The young Edwards spent most of the winter there. The elder Edwards considered Johnson as "a man of not much religion."[50] What a contrast Johnson's home would have been to the home in which the younger Edwards had been raised, where there was a distinct desire that godly piety reign.

One final point needs to be made in this regard. The goal of family life for Edwards and his wife was the enjoyment of God. As Edwards once said:

> The enjoyment of God is the only happiness with which our souls can be satisfied. To go to heaven, fully to enjoy God, is infinitely better than the most pleasant accommodations here. Fathers and mothers, husbands, wives, or children, or the company of earthly friends, are but shadows; but God is the substance. These are but scattered beams, but God is the sun. These are but streams, but God is the fountain. These are but drops; but God is the ocean.[51]

---

50. James Thomas Flexner, *Mohawk Baronet: A Biography of Sir William Johnson* (1959 ed.; repr. Syracuse: Syracuse University Press, 1989), 290.

51. *The Christian Pilgrim* (*Works of Jonathan Edwards*, rev. and corr. Hickman, 2:244).

Other Expressions of Piety

Edwards' God-centered vision, so evident in the text just quoted, bore fruit in a couple of powerful revivals in the church at Northampton as well as in New England as a whole.[52] The second of these revivals, namely the Great Awakening, was not, however, without its critics, many of whom had been deeply impacted by the worldview of the eighteenth-century Enlightenment and thus sought to write the revival off as sheer "enthusiasm" (i.e. fanaticism). Edwards profoundly disagreed with this interpretation, though he was not slow to critique theological and practical aberrations when they appeared during and in the wake of the revival. In the midst of the revival he thus wrote a number of works that sought to defend it as a genuine work of God but which also sought to correct problems that had emerged.[53] Edwards' defense is also very evident in a number of the letters contained in this volume.[54]

Vital for revival and the expansion of God's kingdom was, in Edwards' opinion, corporate prayer. What would become known as the Concert of Prayer, which originated in Scotland among Edwards' Scottish correspondents,[55] was something Edwards "heartily" wished "fallen in with by all Christians from the rising to the setting sun."[56] When Edwards received

---

52. For references to these revivals, see below, pages 50-52, 57.

53. For this defense, see Haykin, *Jonathan Edwards: The Holy Spirit in Revival*.

54. See below, pages 57-60, 88-91.

55. See below, pages 85-86, 91.

56. See below, page 86.

information regarding this prayer movement, he lost no time in seeking to implement a similar concert of prayer in the New England colonies. He encouraged his own congregation to get involved, and also communicated the concept of such a prayer union to neighboring ministers whom he felt would be receptive to the idea.[57]

Although the idea initially met with a poor response, Edwards was not to be put off. In a sermon given in February, 1747, on Zechariah 8:20-22, he sought to demonstrate how the text supported his call for a union of praying Christians. Within the year a revised and greatly expanded version of this sermon was ready for publication as *An Humble Attempt to Promote Explicit Agreement and Visible Union of God's People in Extraordinary Prayer, For the Revival of Religion and the Advancement of Christ's Kingdom on Earth, pursuant to Scripture-Promises and Prophecies concerning the Last Time* (henceforth referred to simply as the *Humble Attempt*). The treatise is well summed up by a sentence near the beginning of the work:

> It is a very suitable thing, and well-pleasing to God, for many people, in different parts of the world, by express agreement, to come into a visible union in extraordinary, speedy, fervent, and constant prayer, for those great effusions of the Holy Spirit, which shall bring on that advancement of Christ's church and kingdom, that God has so often promised shall be in the latter ages of the world.[58]

---

57. See below, pages 85-86.

58. *Humble Attempt* (*Jonathan Edwards: Apocalyptic Writings*, ed.

In essence, the *Humble Attempt* is a call for a practical expression of Reformation theology, which maintains that only God is able to do the work of God.[59] Believing this, the church has only one posture: prayer.

Within two years of writing this treatise on corporate prayer, his church, where Edwards would have longed to have seen his ideas put into practice, had dismissed him. After his dismissal Edwards became the pastor of the church in what was then the frontier village of Stockbridge, Massachusetts. During his time in Stockbridge in the heart of the Berkshire Mountains of Massachusetts, Edwards served as a missionary to some 250 Mohican and 60 Mohawk Indians.[60] Clear evidence from a literary perspective that his missionary life in Stockbridge has not been appreciated is the fact that up until 1999, not one of the sermons that he preached to the Stockbridge Indians had been published.[61] Yet, as George Marsden

---

Stephen J. Stein, vol. 5 of *The Works of Jonathan Edwards* [New Haven/London: Yale University Press, 1977], 320).

59. Robert O. Bakke, *The Power of Extraordinary Prayer* (Wheaton, Illinois: Crossway Books, 2000), 123.

60. See Stephen J. Nichols, "Last of the Mohican Missionaries: Jonathan Edwards at Stockbridge" in D.G. Hart, Sean Michael Lucas, and Stephen J. Nichols, ed., *The Legacy of Jonathan Edwards: American Religion and the Evangelical Tradition* (Grand Rapids, Michigan: Baker, 2003), 47-63.

61. For two of the sermons to the Stockbridge Indians that have been published, see "To the Mohawks at the Treaty, August 16, 1751" and "He That Believeth Shall Be Saved" in Wilson H. Kimnach, Kenneth P. Minkema, and Douglas A. Sweeney, eds., *The Sermons of Jonathan Edwards: A Reader* (New Haven/London: Yale University Press, 1999), 105-120.

has noted, Edwards' pre-eminent goal during his time at Stockbridge was to reach these Indians with the life-giving Gospel.[62] And, as Ron Davies has shown,[63] Edwards' theological vision was increasingly a global one, in which, as he looked to the future, he saw ever-increasing victories in the missionary advance of the kingdom of Christ.

Edwards' removal from Northampton to Stock-bridge was also providential in that he had time to write two notable defenses of Calvinism, which he had been long wanting to write: *A Careful and Strict Inquiry into the Modern Prevailing Notions of that Freedom of the Will, Which is Supposed to be Essential to Moral Agency* (1754) and *The Great Christian Doctrine of Original Sin Defended* (1758).[64]

This period of missionary endeavor and literary fruitfulness at Stockbridge came to an end in 1757, though, when Edwards reluctantly accepted an invitation to become president of the College of New Jersey, now Princeton University.[65]

Edwards arrived in Princeton in late January 1758 and had been at the College only a few weeks when

---

62. Marsden, 408-409.

63. See his "Prepare Ye the Way of the Lord: The Missiological Thought and Practice of Jonathan Edwards (1703-1758)" (Unpublished Ph.D. thesis, Fuller Theological Seminary, 1989); "Jonathan Edwards: Missionary Biographer, Theologian, Strategist, Administrator, Advocate—and Missionary," *International Bulletin of Missionary Research*, 21, no. 2 (April 1997): 60-67; "Jonathan Edwards, theologian of the missionary awakening" (EMA Occasional paper, no. 3 [Spring 1999]) in *Evangel*, 17, no. 1 (Spring 1999); *A Heart for Mission: Five Pioneer Thinkers* (Fearn, Tain, Ross-shire: Christian Focus, 2002), 79-96.

64. For evidence of this, see below, pages 97-98, 148-149.

65. See below, pages 145-152.

he was inoculated against smallpox, which was raging in Princeton and the vicinity. The vaccine initially appeared to be successful, but complications set in, and Edwards, never a strong man physically, died on March 22, 1758.[66] To his two children who were present at his bedside, Esther and Lucy (1736-1786), he said a little before his death:

> It seems to me to be the will of God that I must shortly leave you; therefore give my kindest love to my dear wife, and tell her, that the uncommon union, which has so long subsisted between us, has been of such a nature, as I trust is spiritual, and therefore will continue forever: and I hope she shall be supported under so great a trial, and submit cheerfully to the will of God. And as to my children, you are now like to be left fatherless, which I hope will be an inducement to you all to seek a Father, who will never fail you.[67]

Just before his death, those at his bedside, supposing he was unconscious, were lamenting what his death would mean to the college and to the church, when they were surprised by what proved to be his last words: "Trust in God, and ye need not fear."[68] To the end Edwards maintained a God-centered focus: the living God was all-sufficient and would ever care

---

66. For letters relating to his death, see below, pages 155-159.

67. "Life and Character of the Late Reverend Mr. Jonathan Edwards" in Levin, ed., *Jonathan Edwards*, 80.

68. Cited Hopkins, "Life and Character of the Late Reverend Mr. Jonathan Edwards" in Levin, ed., *Jonathan Edwards*, 81.

for His Church.[69] Or as Edwards wrote to one of his friends when her son had just died:

> Therefore, in this we may be confident, though the earth be removed, in him we shall triumph with everlasting joy. Now, when storms and tempests arise, we may resort to him, who is a hiding-place from the storm, and a covert from the tempest....[And h]aving found him, who is as the apple-tree among the trees of the wood, we may sit under his shadow with great delight, and his fruit will be sweet to our taste.[70]

---

69. See the remarks of Hopkins, "Life and Character of the Late Reverend Mr. Jonathan Edwards" in Levin, ed., *Jonathan Edwards*, 81.

70. See below, page 130.

1

To Mary Edwards[1]

Windsor, May 10, 1716

Dear sister,

Through the wonderful goodness and mercy of God, there has been in this place a very remarkable outpouring of the Spirit of God. It still continues, but I think I have reason to think is in some measure diminished, yet I hope not much. Thirteen have joined the church since you last heard; five now stand propounded for admission; and I think above thirty persons come commonly on Mondays to converse with father about the condition of their souls.[2] It is a time of general health here. Abigail, Hannah, and Lucy have had the chicken pox and are recovered. Jerusha is almost well.[3] Except her, the whole family is well.

---

1. From "Memoirs," xvi. This is the earliest letter we have from Edwards, written when he was twelve years of age. Mary Edwards (1701-1776) was one of his older sisters.

2. In the version that appears in the "Memoirs" it says "three" had joined the church. But in the critical edition of this letter in *Letters and Personal Writings*, 29, it says "thirteen." The "three" of the "Memoirs" probably originated in the fact that the young Edwards names three people that his sister had not heard about becoming members of the church.

3. These were sisters of Edwards: Abigail (1707-1764), Hannah (1713-1773), Lucy (1715-1736), and Jerusha (1710-1729). See

Sister, I am glad to hear of your welfare so often as I do, I should be glad to hear from you by letter, and therein how it is with you as to your crookedness.

Your loving brother,

Jonathan E.

Marsden, 510. For a study of his sisters, see Kenneth P. Minkema, "Hannah and Her Sisters: Sisterhood, Courtship, and Marriage in the Edwards Family in the Early Eighteenth Century," *The New England Historical and Genealogical Register*, 146 (January 1992): 35-56. See also Marsden, 18-19.

2

To Benjamin Colman[1]

Northampton, March 19, 1737

We in this town were, the last Lord's day (March 13th,) the spectators, and many of us the subjects, of one of the most amazing instances of divine preservation, that perhaps was ever known in the world. Our meetinghouse is old and decayed, so that we have been for some time building a new one, which is yet unfinished. It has been observed of late that the house

---

1. From "Memoirs," xlix-1. For Colman as the most probable recipient of this letter, see *Letters and Personal Writings*, 64-65. Benjamin Colman (1673-1747) was the pastor of the Brattle Street Church, Boston. He was a prolific author who had more than ninety books published. He played an important role in the publication of Edwards' *A Faithful Narrative of the Surprising Work of God* (1737). For his life, see Ebenezer Turell, *The Life and Character of the Reverend Benjamin Colman, D.D.* (1749 ed.; repr. Delmar, New York: Scholars' Facsimiles & Reprints, 1972). For a brief overview of Colman as a preacher and of worship in his congregation, see Hughes Oliphant Old, *The Reading and Preaching of the Scriptures in the Worship of the Christian Church. Vol. 5: Moderatism, Pietism, and Awakening* (Grand Rapids/Cambridge, U.K.: William B. Eerdmans Publ. Co., 2004), 244-247.

In this letter Edwards describes the collapse of the gallery of the congregation's second meeting-house and the providence attending this event. The meeting-house had been in use since the early 1660s. As Edwards notes, this meeting-house was in a decrepit shape, and its demise was hastened by the particularly severe winter of 1736-1737. The third meeting-house was not ready until January 1738. See Marsden, 184-189.

Benjamin Colman (1673-1747)

(The frontispiece to Ebenezer Turell, *The Life and Character of the Reverend Benjamin Colman, D.D.* [1749 ed.; repr. Delmar, New York: Scholars' Facsimiles & Reprints, 1972])

we have hitherto met in has gradually spread at the bottom, the sills and walls giving way, especially in the foreside, by reason of the weight of timber at top pressing on the braces that are inserted into the posts and beams of the house. It has done so more than ordinarily this spring, which seems to have been occasioned by the heaving of the ground, through the extreme frosts of the winter past, and its now settling again on that side which is next the sun, by the spring thaws. By this means, the underpinning has been considerably disordered, which people were not sensible of till the ends of the joists, which bore up the front gallery, were drawn off from the girts on which they rested, by the walls giving way. So that in the midst of the public exercise in the forenoon, soon after the beginning of the sermon, the whole gallery—full of people, with all the seats and timbers, suddenly, and without any warning—sunk, and fell down, with the most amazing noise, upon the heads of those that sat under, to the astonishment of the congregation. The house was filled with dolorous shrieking and crying; and nothing else was expected than to find many people dead, or dashed to pieces.

The gallery, in falling, seemed to break and sink first in the middle, so that those who were upon it were thrown together in heaps before the front door. But the whole was so sudden that many of those who fell knew nothing what it was, at the time, that had befallen them. Others in the congregation thought it had been an amazing clap of thunder. The falling gallery seemed to be broken all to pieces before it got down, so that some who fell with it, as well as those who were under, were buried in the ruins, and were found pressed under heavy loads of timber, and could do nothing to help themselves.

But so mysteriously and wonderfully did it come to pass that every life was preserved, and though many were greatly bruised and their flesh torn, yet there is not, as I can understand, one bone broken, or so much as put out of joint, among them all. Some, who were thought to be almost dead at first, are greatly recovered; and but one young woman seems yet to remain in dangerous circumstances, by an inward hurt in her breast; but of late there appears more hope of her recovery.

None can give an account, or conceive, by what means people's lives and limbs should be thus preserved, when so great a multitude were thus imminently exposed. It looked as though it was impossible but that great numbers must instantly be crushed to death or dashed in pieces. It seems unreasonable to ascribe it to anything else but the care of Providence in disposing the motions of every piece of timber and the precise place of safety where everyone should sit and fall, when none were in any capacity to care for their own preservation. The preservation seems to be most wonderful with respect to the women and children in the middle alley under the gallery, where it came down first and with greatest force, and where there was nothing to break the force of the falling weight.

Such an event may be a sufficient argument of a Divine providence over the lives of men. We thought ourselves called on to set apart a day to be spent in the solemn worship of God, to humble ourselves under such a rebuke of God upon us, in time of public service in his house, by so dangerous and surprising an accident, and to praise his name for so wonderful, and as it were miraculous, a preservation. The last Wednesday was kept by us to that end; and a mercy, in which the hand of God is so remarkably evident, may be well worthy to affect the hearts of all who hear it.

George Whitefield (1714-1770)

3

To George Whitefield[1]

Northampton in New-England   February 12, 1740
Rev. Sir,

    My request to you is, that in your intended jour-
ney through New England the next summer, you
would be pleased to visit Northampton. I hope it
is not wholly from curiosity that I desire to see and
hear you in this place. But I apprehend, from what I
have heard, that you are one that has the blessing of
Heaven attending you wherever you go; and I have

    1. From H. Abelove, "Jonathan Edwards' Letter of Invitation to
George Whitefield," *William and Mary Quarterly*, Series 3, 29 (1972):
488-489. Reproduced with permission.

    George Whitefield (1714-1770) was the leading evangelist of the
eighteenth century, who typified the zeal and fervor of the transatlantic Evangelical revivals. For his life, see especially Arnold Dallimore,
*George Whitefield: The Life and Times of the Great Evangelist of the Eigh-
teenth-Century Revival*, 2 vols. (1970 and 1979 eds.; repr. Westchester,
Illinois: Cornerstone Books, 1979 and 1980).

    See also the following studies of his life and thought, David
Crump, "The Preaching of George Whitefield and His Use of Mat-
thew Henry's *Commentary*," *Crux*, 25, no. 3 (September 1989): 19-28;
James M. Gordon, *Evangelical Spirituality* (London: SPCK, 1991),
53-66; J. I. Packer, "The Spirit with the Word: The Reformational
Revivalism of George Whitefield" in W. P. Stephens, ed., *The Bible,
the Reformation and the Church. Essays in Honour of James Atkinson*
(Sheffield: Sheffield Academic Press, 1995), 166-189; and Michael
A.G. Haykin, *The revived Puritan: The spirituality of George Whitefield*
(Dundas, Ontario: Joshua Press, 2000).

a great desire, if it may be the will of God, that such a blessing as attends your person and labors may descend on this town, and may enter mine own house, and that I may receive it in my own soul. Indeed I am fearful whether you will not be disappointed in New England, and will have less success here than in other places. We who have dwelt in the land that has been distinguished with Light, and have long enjoyed the Gospel, and have been glutted with it, and have despised it, are I fear more hardened than most of those places where you have preached hitherto. But yet I hope in that power and mercy of God that has appeared so triumphant in the success of your labors in other places, that he will send a blessing with you even to us, tho' we are unworthy of it.

I hope, if God preserves my life, to see something of that salvation of God in New England which he has now begun, in the benighted, wicked and miserable world and age and in the most guilty of all nations. It has been with refreshment of soul that I have heard of one raised up in the Church of England to revive the mysterious, spiritual, despised and exploded[2] doctrines of the Gospel, and full of a Spirit of zeal for the promotion of real vital piety, whose labors have been attended with such success. Blessed be God that hath done it! who is with you, and helps you, and makes the weapons of your warfare mighty.

We see that God is faithful, and never will forget the promises that he has made to his Church; and that he will not suffer the smoking flax to be quenched, even when the floods seem to be overwhelming it, but

---

2. By "exploded," Edwards means "discredited."

will revive the flame again, even in the darkest times. I hope this is the dawning of a day of God's mighty power and glorious grace to the world of mankind. May you go on Rev. Sir! And may God be with you more and more abundantly that the work of God may be carried on by a blessing on your labours still, with that swift progress that it has been hitherto, and rise to a greater height, and extend further and further, with an irresistible power bearing down all opposition! And may the gates of Hell never be able to prevail against you! And may God send forth more laborers into his harvest of a like Spirit, until the Kingdom of Satan shall shake, and his proud Empire fall throughout the earth and the Kingdom of Christ, that glorious Kingdom of light, holiness, peace and love, shall be established from one end of the earth unto the other!

Give my love to Mr. Seward.[3] I hope to see him here with you. I believe I may venture to say that what has been heard of your labors and success has not been taken notice of more in any place in New England than here, or received with fuller credit. I hope therefore if we have opportunity, we shall hear you with greater attention. The way from New York to Boston through Northampton is but little further

---

3. William Seward (1711-1740) acted as Whitefield's business manager during this evangelistic tour of America. Seward was a man of wealth and supported the tour generously out of his own funds. He returned to England in April 1740, and thus never met Edwards. He died from mob violence in Wales while traveling that October with the Welsh evangelist Howell Harris (1714-1773). See W.R. Ward, "Seward, William" in Donald M. Lewis, ed., *The Blackwell Dictionary of Evangelical Biography 1730-1860* (Oxford: Blackwell Publishers, 1995), II, 996. Edwards actually called him "Sewart."

than the nearest that is; and I think leads through as populous a part of the Country as any. I desire that you and Mr. Seward would come directly to my house. I shall account it a great favor and smile of Providence to have opportunity to entertain such guests under my roof, and to have some acquaintance with such persons.[4]

I fear it is too much for me to desire a particular remembrance in your prayers, when I consider how many thousands do doubtless desire it, who can't all be particularly mentioned; and I am far from thinking myself worthy to be distinguished. But pray Sir, let your heart be lifted up to God for me among others, that God would bestow much of that blessed Spirit on me that he has bestowed on you, and make me also an instrument of his Glory. I am Rev. Sir,

> unworthy to be called your fellow laborer,
> Jonathan Edwards.

---

4. For the actual visit, see below, pages 63-64.

4

To Deborah Hatheway[1]

Northampton, June 3, 1741

My dear young friend,

As you desired me to send you, in writing, some directions how to conduct yourself in your Christian course, I would now answer your request. The sweet remembrance of the great things I have lately seen at Suffield inclines me to do anything in my power to contribute to the spiritual joy and prosperity of God's people there.

---

1. From "Memoirs," liii-liv. Deborah Hatheway (1722-1753) was living in Suffield, Massachusetts, when she received this letter. She had been converted in a revival that had come to the town in the spring of 1741, possibly as a result of a visit by Edwards in April of that year. Hatheway turned to Edwards for advice about how to live the Christian life since her church was without a pastor. This letter was often reprinted in the nineteenth century and became something of a minor classic of spiritual advice. By 1875 at least 328,000 copies of this letter had been printed.

In the original version, the letter has nineteen pieces of advice, most of which center upon growth in humility and holiness, and the cultivation of a deep sense of gratitude to God for forgiveness and salvation. Of the two that have been left out, one is quite similar to #12 below. The other urged Deborah not to "talk of things of religion and matters of experience with an air of lightness and laughter" (*Letters and Personal Writings*, 95).

For a modern edition of this letter, see *Jonathan Edwards' Resolutions and Advice to Young Converts*, ed. Stephen J. Nichols (Phillipsburg, New Jersey: P&R Publishing, 2001).

1. I would advise you to keep up as great a strife and earnestness in religion as if you knew yourself to be in a state of nature and were seeking conversion. We advise persons under conviction to be earnest and violent for the kingdom of heaven; but when they have attained to conversion, they ought not to be the less watchful, laborious, and earnest in the whole work of religion, but the more so; for they are under infinitely greater obligations. For want of this, many persons, in a few months after their conversion, have begun to lose their sweet and lively sense of spiritual things, and to grow cold and dark, and have "pierced themselves through with many sorrows."[2] Whereas, if they had done as the apostle did (Philippians 3:12-14), their path would have been "as the shining light, that shines more and more unto the perfect day."[3]

2. Do not leave off seeking, striving, and praying for the very same things that we exhort unconverted persons to strive for, and a degree of which you have had already in conversion. Pray that your eyes may be opened, that you may receive sight, that you may know yourself, and be brought to God's footstool; and that you may see the glory of God and Christ, and may be raised from the dead, and have the love of Christ shed abroad in your heart. Those who have most of these things, have need still to pray for them; for there is so much blindness and hardness, pride and death remaining that they still need to have that work of God wrought upon them, further to enlighten and enliven them, that shall be bringing

---

2. 1 Timothy 6:10.

3. Proverbs 4:18.

them out of darkness into God's marvelous light, and be a kind of new conversion and resurrection from the dead. There are very few requests that are proper for an impenitent man, that are not also, in some sense, proper for the godly.

3. When you hear a sermon, hear for yourself. Though what is spoken may be more especially directed to the unconverted, or to those that, in other respects, are in different circumstances from yourself, yet, let the chief intent of your mind be to consider, "In what respect is this applicable to me? And what improvement ought I to make of this, for my own soul's good?"

4. Though God has forgiven and forgotten your past sins, yet do not forget them yourself: often remember, what a wretched bond-slave you were in the land of Egypt. Often bring to mind your particular acts of sin before conversion, as the blessed apostle Paul is often mentioning his old blaspheming, persecuting spirit, and his injuriousness to the renewed, humbling his heart, and acknowledging that he was "the least of the apostles," and not worthy "to be called an apostle," and the "least of all saints," and the "chief of sinners."[4] And be often confessing your old sins to God, and let that text be often in your mind, "That thou mayest remember and be confounded, and never open thy mouth any more, because of thy shame, when I am pacified toward thee for all that thou hast done, saith the Lord God" (Ezekiel 16:63).

5. Remember, that you have more cause, on some accounts a thousand times, to lament and humble

---

4. 1 Corinthians 15:9; Ephesians 3:8; 1 Timothy 1:15.

yourself for sins that have been committed since conversion than before, because of the infinitely greater obligations that are upon you to live to God, and to look upon the faithfulness of Christ, in unchangeably continuing his loving-kindness, notwithstanding all your great unworthiness since your conversion.

6. Be always greatly abased for your remaining sin and never think that you lie low enough for it. But yet be not discouraged or disheartened by it, for, though we are exceeding sinful, yet "we have an advocate with the Father, Jesus Christ the righteous,"[5] the preciousness of whose blood, the merit of whose righteousness, and the greatness of whose love and faithfulness, infinitely overtop the highest mountains of our sins.

7. When you engage in the duty of prayer, or come to the Lord's supper, or attend any other duty of divine worship, come to Christ as Mary Magdalen (Luke 7:37-38)[6] did come, and cast yourself at his feet, and kiss them, and pour forth upon him the sweet perfumed ointment of divine love, out of a pure and broken heart, as she poured the precious ointment out of her pure broken alabaster box.

8. Remember that pride is the worst viper that is in the heart, the greatest disturber of the soul's peace and of sweet communion with Christ. It was the first sin committed and lies lowest in the foundation of Satan's whole building, and is with the greatest difficulty rooted out, and is the most hidden, secret, and

---

5. 1 John 2:2.

6. Edwards here is following a common exegetical tradition that regarded Mary Magdalene as the woman in Luke 7.

deceitful of all lusts, and often creeps insensibly into the midst of religion, even, sometimes, under the disguise of humility itself.

9. That you may pass a correct judgment concerning yourself, always look upon those as the best discoveries, and the best comforts, that have most of these two effects: those that make you least and lowest, and most like a child; and those that most engage and fix your heart, in a full and firm disposition to deny yourself for God, and to spend and be spent for him.

10. If at any time you fall into doubts about the state of your soul, in dark and dull frames of mind, it is proper to review your past experience. But do not consume too much time and strength in this way; rather apply yourself, with all your might, to an earnest pursuit after renewed experience, new light, and new lively acts of faith and love. One new discovery of the glory of Christ's face will do more toward scattering clouds of darkness in one minute, than examining old experience, by the best marks that can be given, through a whole year.

11. When the exercise of grace is low, and corruption prevails, and by that means fear prevails, do not desire to have fear cast out any other way than by the reviving and prevailing of love in the heart. By this, fear will be effectually expelled, as darkness in a room vanishes away when the pleasant beams of the sun are let into it.

12. When you counsel and warn others, do it earnestly and affectionately and thoroughly. And when you are speaking to your equals, let your warnings be intermixed with expressions of your sense of your

own unworthiness and of the sovereign grace that makes you differ.

13. If you would set up religious meetings of young women by yourselves, to be attended once in a while, besides the other meetings that you attend, I should think it would be very proper and profitable.

14. Under special difficulties, or when in great need of or great longings after any particular mercy for yourself or others, set apart a day for secret prayer and fasting by yourself alone; and let the day be spent, not only in petitions for the mercies you desire, but in searching your heart, and in looking over your past life, and confessing your sins before God, not as is wont to be done in public prayer, but by a very particular rehearsal before God of the sins of your past life, from your childhood hitherto, before and after conversion, with the circumstances and aggravations attending them, and spreading all the abominations of your heart very particularly, and fully as possible, before him.

15. Do not let the adversaries of the cross have occasion to reproach religion on your account. How holily should the children of God, the redeemed and the beloved of the Son of God, behave themselves. Therefore, "walk as children of the light" and of the day and "adorn the doctrine of God your Savior."[7] And especially abound in what are called the Christian virtues and make you like the Lamb of God: be meek and lowly of heart, and full of pure, heavenly, and humble love to all; abound in deeds of love to others, and self-denial for others; and let there be

---

7. See Ephesians 5:8; Titus 2:10.

in you a disposition to account others better than yourself.

16. In all your course, walk with God and follow Christ, as a little, poor, helpless child, taking hold of Christ's hand, keeping your eye on the marks of the wounds in his hands and side, whence came the blood that cleanses you from sin, and hiding your nakedness under the skirt of the white shining robes of his righteousness.

17. Pray much for the ministers and the church of God, especially, that he would carry on his glorious work which he has now begun, till the world shall be full of his glory.

A nineteenth-century print of George Whitefield
preaching during the Great Awakening.

5

To Sarah Edwards, Jr.[1]

Northampton, June 25, 1741

My dear child,

Your mother has received two letters from you, since you went away. We rejoice to hear of your welfare and of the flourishing state of religion in Lebanon. I hope you will well improve the great advantage God is thereby putting into your hands, for the good of your own soul. You have very weak and infirm health, and I am afraid are always like to have; and it may be, are not to be long-lived; and while you do live, are not like to enjoy so much of the comforts of this life as others do, by reason of your want of health; and therefore, if you have no better portion, will be miserable indeed. But, if your soul prospers, you will be a happy, blessed person, whatever becomes of your body. I wish you much of the presence of Christ, and of communion with him, and that you might live so as to give him honor, in the place where you are, by an amiable behavior towards all.

---

1. From "Memoirs," liii. Sarah Edwards was Jonathan's eldest daughter. She was staying with an aunt and uncle in Lebanon, Connecticut, when her father wrote her this letter. See *Letters and Personal Writings*, 95. See above, pages 13-14, and for another reference to Sarah, after her marriage to Elihu Parsons, see below, page 134.

...The flourishing of religion in this town, and in these parts of the country has rather increased since you went away.[2] Your mother joins with me in giving her love to you, and to your uncle and aunt. Your sisters give their love to you and their duty to them. The whole family is glad, when we hear from you. Recommending you to the continual care and mercy of heaven, I remain your loving father,

Jonathan Edwards.

---

2. A reference to the Great Awakening of 1740-1742.

6

To Joseph Bellamy[1]

Northampton, January 21, 1742

Rev. and dear Sir,

I received yours of January 11, for which I thank you. Religion, in this and the neighboring towns, has now of late been on the decaying hand. I desire your prayers that God would quicken and revive us again; and particularly that he would greatly humble, and pardon, and quicken me, and fill me with his own fullness; and, if it may consist with his will, improve me as an instrument to revive his work. There has been, the year past, the most wonderful work among children here, by far, that ever was. God has seemed

---

1. From "Memoirs," lvi. Joseph Bellamy (1719-1790) was both a follower and close friend of Edwards. He ministered at Bethlehem, Connecticut, from 1740 till his death. On one occasion Edwards described him as "one of the most intimate friends" that he had (Letter to John Erskine, July 5, 1750 ["Memoirs," cxviii]). See below, page 117.

For a recent study on Bellamy, see Mark Valeri, *Law and Providence in Joseph Bellamy's New England: The Origins of the New Divinity in Revolutionary America* (New York: Oxford University Press, 1994). For a brief overview of his life and work, see James P. Walsh, "Bellamy, Joseph," *American National Biography* (New York/Oxford: Oxford University Press, 1999), 2:522-523. For a couple of selections from his works, see Douglas A. Sweeney and Allen C. Guelzo, eds., *The New England Theology: From Jonathan Edwards to Edwards Amasa Park* (Grand Rapids: Baker, 2006), 73-85.

almost wholly to take a new generation that is come on since the late great work, seven years ago.

Neither earth nor hell can hinder his work that is going on in the country. Christ gloriously triumphs at this day. You have probably before now heard of the great and wonderful things that have lately been wrought at Portsmouth, the chief town in New Hampshire. There are also appearing great things at Ipswich and Newbury, the two largest towns in this province except Boston, and several other towns beyond Boston, and some towns nearer. By what I can understand, the work of God is greater at this day in the land than it has been at any time. O what cause have we, with exulting hearts, to agree to give glory to him, who thus rides forth in the chariot of his salvation, conquering and to conquer; and earnestly to pray, that now the Sun of righteousness would come forth like a bridegroom, rejoicing as a giant, to run his race from one end of the heavens to the other, that nothing may be hid from the light and heat thereof.[2]

It is not probable that I shall be able to attend your meeting at Guilford. I have lately been so much gone from my people, and don't know but I must be obliged to leave 'em again next week about a fortnight, being called to Leicester, a town about half way to Boston, where a great work of grace has lately commenced, and probably soon after that to another place, and having at this time some extraordinary affairs to attend to at home.[3] I pray that Christ, our

---

2. Edwards is referring to Malachi 4:2 and Psalm 19:4-6.

3. This paragraph indicates that while Edwards was not an itiner-

good Shepherd, will be with you, and direct you and greatly strengthen and bless you....

I am, dear Sir, your affectionate and unworthy brother, and fellow-laborer,

Jonathan Edwards.

---

ant preacher like George Whitefield, he did preach in various places throughout New England during the time of the Great Awakening.

7

---•◦(◦)◦•---

To James Robe[1]

Northampton, May 12, 1743

Rev. and dear Sir,

Last week I was surprised with the unexpected favor of your letter, with one from Mr. MacLaurin.[2]

---

1. From *The Christian Monthly History*, 2 (1745), 127-130. James Robe (1688-1753) was the Presbyterian minister of Kilsyth, Scotland and had seen revival in his parish in 1740. See C.W. Mitchell, "Robe, James," *Oxford Dictionary of National Biography*, eds. H. C. G. Matthew and Brian Harrison (Oxford: Oxford University Press, 2004), 47:76.

For Edwards' correspondence with various Scottish ministers, see Christopher W. Mitchell, "Jonathan Edwards's Scottish Connection" in David W. Kling and Douglas A. Sweeney, eds., *Jonathan Edwards at Home and Abroad: Historical Memories, Cultural Movements, Global Horizons* (Columbia, South Carolina: University of South Carolina Press, 2003), 222-247 and D.W. Bebbington, "The reputation of Edwards abroad" in Stephen J. Stein, ed., *The Cambridge Companion to Jonathan Edwards* (Cambridge: Cambridge University Press, 2007), 240-241. Mitchell points out that Edwards and his Scottish correspondents shared a mutual passion for "true religion" and for its re-establishment in its pristine form of evangelical Calvinism. For some details about Edwards' correspondence with Robe, see Mitchell, "Jonathan Edwards's Scottish Connection," 228-229.

2. John MacLaurin (1693-1754) was a prominent Scottish Presbyterian minister, the pastor of the Ramshorn Church in northwest Glasgow from 1723 to 1754. See Mitchell, "Jonathan Edwards's Scottish Connection," 227-228. According to Dwight ("Memoirs," lxxii), it was MacLaurin who made the first contact with Edwards and so initiated Edwards' epistolary links with various Scottish

It may well make me blush at the consideration of my vileness, to receive such undeserved testimonies of respect from servants of the Lord, at so great a distance, and that have been so highly favored and honored of God as you have been. Pleasant and joyful are the accounts which we have lately had from Scotland, concerning the kingdom of our God there, for which we and the world are specially indebted to you, who have honored your dear Lord, and refreshed and served his church, by the accounts you have published in your narrative and journals of the work of God in Kilsyth, and other parts in the West of Scotland.[3] Future generations will own themselves indebted to you for those accounts. I congratulate you, dear Sir, on the advantages God has put you under to favor the church of God with a narrative of his glorious works, by having made you the instrument of so much of them, and giving you such glorious success in your own congregation. The accounts which we have received from you are, on some accounts, more pleasant and agreeable than what we have had to send to you. The work of God with you has been less mixed with error and extravagance; you have taken a more wise and prudent care to prevent things of that nature, or to suppress them as soon as they have appeared; and ministers that

---

ministers. For a brief biographical sketch of MacLaurin, see James Ramsay Macdonald, "MacLaurin, John," *The Compact Edition of the Dictionary of National Biography* (London: Oxford University Press, 1975), I, 1286.

3. Edwards is referring to James Robe's *A Faithful Narrative of the Extraordinary Work of the Spirit of God at Kilsyth, and Other Congregations in the Neighborhood near Glasgow* (Glasgow, 1742).

have been the principal promoters of the work have seemed to be more happily united in their sentiments, and so under greater advantage to assist one another, and to act as co-workers and fellow helpers.

You have heard great things from New England of late, which, I doubt not, have refreshed and rejoiced your hearts; and indeed, great and wonderful have the things been in which God has passed before us. But now we have not such joyful news to send you. The clouds have lately thickened and our hemisphere is now much darkened with them. There is a great decay of the work of God amongst us, especially as to the awakening and converting influence of the Spirit of God; and the prejudices there are, in a great part of the country, are riveted and inveterate. The people are divided into two parties, those that favor the work and those that are against it, and the distinction has long been growing more and more visible, and the distance greater, till there is at length raised a wall between them up to heaven; so that one party is very much out of the reach of all influence of the other. This is very much owing to imprudent management in the friends of the work, and a corrupt mixture which Satan has found means to introduce, and our manifold sinful errors by which we have grieved and quenched the Spirit of God.

It can scarcely be conceived of what consequence it is, to the continuance and propagation of a revival of religion, that the utmost care be used to prevent error and disorder among those that appear to be the subjects of such a work. As also that all imaginable care be taken by ministers in conducting souls under the work; and particularly that there be the greatest caution used in comforting and establishing persons as being safe and past danger of hell. Many among us have been ready to think that all high raptures are divine; but experience plainly shows that it is not the degree of rapture and ecstasy (though it should be to the third heavens), but the nature and kind that must determine us in their favor. It would have been better for us, if all ministers here had taken care diligently to distinguish such joys and raised affections, as were attended with deep humiliation, brokenness of heart, poverty of spirit, mourning for sin, solemnity of spirit, a trembling reverence towards God, tenderness of spirit, self-jealousy and fear, and great engagedness of heart after holiness of life, and a readiness to esteem others better than themselves; and that sort of humility that is not a noisy showy humility, but rather this which disposes to walk softly and speak trembling. And if we had encouraged no discoveries or joys but such as manifestly wrought this way, it would have been well for us.

And I am persuaded we shall generally be sensible, before long, that we run too fast when we endeavor by our positive determinations to banish all fears of damnation from the minds of men, though they may be true saints, if they are not such as are eminently humble and mortified, and (what the Apostle calls) "rooted and grounded in love" [Ephesians 3:17]. It seems to be running before the Spirit of God. God by his Spirit does not give assurance any other way, than by advancing these things in the soul. He does not wholly cast out fear, the legal principle, but by advancing and filling the soul full of love, the evangelical principle. When love is low in the true saints, they need the fear of hell to deter them from sin, and engage them to exactness in their walk, and stir them up to seek heaven. But when love is high, and the soul full of it, we don't need fear. And therefore a wise God has so ordered it that love and fear should rise and fall like the scales of a balance. When one rises, the other falls, as there is need, or as light and darkness take place of each other in a room, as light decays, darkness comes in, and as light increases and fills the room, darkness is cast out. So love, or the spirit of adoption, casts out fear, the spirit of bondage. And experience convinces me that even in the brightest and most promising appearances of new converts, it would have been better for us to have encouraged them only as it were conditionally, after the example of the Apostle, Hebrews 3:6, "Whose house are we, if we hold fast the confidence and the rejoicing of the hope firm unto the end," and verse 14, "For we are made partakers of Christ, if we hold the beginning of our confidence steadfast unto the end." And after the example of Christ, Revelation 2:10, "Be thou faithful unto death, and I will give thee a crown of life." So Luke 21:34-36, and in many other places. 'Tis probable that one reason why God has suffered us to err is to teach us wisdom by experience of the ill consequence of our errors.

...I have reason to admire divine condescension in making any use of anything I have written for the defense of the work of God in Scotland. As to what you propose concerning my writing a narrative, etc., I am not conveniently situated for it, living in an extreme part of the land, and an hundred miles from the press, as well as on many other accounts unfit for it. But Mr. Prince of Boston, who is every way fit, and under good advantages for it, has already undertaken it, and, I suppose, will prosecute the undertaking, so far as it shall be thought for God's glory.[4]

I hope, dear Sir, you'll remember me in your prayers. Never was I so sensible in any measure how vain a creature man is, what a leaf driven of the wind, what dry stubble, what poor dust, a bubble, a shadow, a nothing, and more vain than nothing, and what a vain and vile helpless creature I am, and how much I need God's help in everything, as of late. Dear Sir, don't forget New England, and don't forget your affectionate and obliged brother and servant, and unworthy fellow laborer,

Jonathan Edwards.

---

4. On Prince, see above, pages 16-17, and n. 43.

8

To Thomas Prince[1]

Northampton, December 12, 1743

Rev. and dear Sir,

Ever since the great work of God, that was wrought here about nine years ago, there has been a great and abiding alteration in this town in many respects.[2] There has been vastly more religion kept up in the town among all sorts of persons, in religious exercises, and in common conversation. There has been a great alteration among the youth of the town with respect to revelry, frolicking, profane and licentious conversation, and lewd songs. And there has also been a great alteration, amongst both old and young, with regard to tavern-haunting. I suppose the town has been in no measure so free of vice in these respects, for any long time together, for sixty years, as it has been these nine years past. There has also been an evident alteration, with respect to a charitable spirit to the poor; though I think with regard to this, we in this town, as well as the land in general, come

---

1. From "Memoirs," lvii-lviii. On Prince, see above, pages 16-17, and n. 43. Prince's daughter, Sarah Prince (1728-1771), was the closest friend of Edwards' daughter Esther. On Esther, see above, pages 14-17.

2. A reference to the Northampton revival of 1734-1735.

Old South Church, Boston, where
Thomas Prince was the minister.

(Henry R. Blaney, *Old Boston: Reproductions of Etchings in Half Tone* [Boston: Lee and Shepard Publishers, 1896], p. 53)

far short of gospel rules.[3] And though after that great work nine years ago, there has been a very lamentable decay of religious affections, and the engagedness of people's spirit in religion, yet many societies for prayer and social worship were all along kept up, and there were some few instances of awakening, and deep concern about the things of another world even in the most dead time.

In the year 1740, in the spring before Mr. Whitefield came to this town, there was a visible alteration. There was more seriousness and religious conversation, especially among young people. Those things that were of ill tendency among them were forborne; and it was a very frequent thing for persons to consult their minister upon the salvation of their souls; and in some particular persons there appeared a great attention about that time. And thus it continued, until Mr. Whitefield came to town, which was about the middle of October following.[4] He preached here four sermons in the meeting-house (besides a private lecture at my house), one on Friday, another on Saturday, and two upon the Sabbath. The congregation was extraordinarily melted by every sermon, almost

---

3. On Edwards' concern for the poor, see Sharon James, "Compassion & Wisdom: The Response of Jonathan Edwards to the Problem of Poverty," *The Baptist Review of Theology*, 5, no. 1 (Spring 1995): 53-62.

4. Whitefield met Edwards for the first time on Friday, October 17, 1740. Whitefield's memorable visit to Northampton lasted until the following Monday, October 20. Of Edwards and his wife Sarah, Whitefield noted in his diary, "a sweeter couple I have not yet seen." See *George Whitefield's Journals* ([London]: The Banner of Truth Trust, 1960), 476-477.

the whole assembly being in tears for a great part of sermon time.[5]

Mr. Whitefield's sermons were suitable to the circumstances of the town, containing a just reproof of our backslidings, and in a most moving and affecting manner, making use of our great professions and great mercies as arguments with us to return to God, from whom we had departed. Immediately after this, the minds of the people in general appeared more engaged in religion, showing a greater forwardness to make religion the subject of their conversation, and to meet frequently for religious purposes, and to embrace all opportunities to hear the word preached. The revival at first appeared chiefly among professors and those that had entertained hope that they were in a state of salvation, to whom Mr. Whitefield chiefly addressed himself. But in a very short time, there appeared an awakening and deep concern among some young persons, that looked upon themselves in a Christless state. And there were some hopeful appearances of conversion and some professors were greatly revived. In about a month or six weeks, there was a great attention in the town, both as to the revival of professors and the awakening of others. By the middle of December, a considerable work of God appeared among those that were very young; and the revival of religion continued to increase, so that in

---

5. According to Whitefield, while he was preaching, "few eyes were dry in the assembly. I had an affecting prospect of the glories of the upper world, and was enabled to speak with some degree of pathos. It seemed as if a time of refreshing was come from the presence of the Lord" (*George Whitefield's Journals*, 476).

the spring an engagedness of spirit about the things of religion was become very general amongst young people and children, and religious subjects almost wholly took up their conversation when they were together.

9

To Elnathan Whitman[1]

Northampton, February 9, 1744

Rev. and dear Sir,

...As to differences among professing Christians...about things that appertain to religion and the worship of God, I am ready to think that you and I are agreed as to the general principles of liberty of conscience, and that men's using methods with their neighbors to oblige them to a conformity to their sentiments or way is in nothing so unreasonable as in the worship of God, because that is a business, in which each person acts for himself, with his Creator and Supreme Judge, as one concerned for his own acceptance with him, and on which depends his own, and not his neighbor's eternal happiness, and salvation from everlasting ruin. And it is an affair, wherein every man is infinitely more concerned with his Creator than he is with his neighbor.

---

1. From "Memoirs," lxxv-lxxvii, *passim*. Elnathan Whitman (1709-1772) was a pastor in Hartford, Connecticut, and the first cousin of Edwards. He had written to Edwards for advice about people who had left his church for another that was pastored by a minister favorable to the Great Awakening. As Claghorn notes, Edwards' response is "a plea for charity and freedom of conscience" (*Letters and Personal Writings*, 127). It reveals Edwards at his best as a wise counselor with regard to church issues.

And so I suppose that it will be allowed, that every man ought to be left to his own conscience, in what he judges will be most acceptable to God, or what he supposes is the will of God, as to the kind, or manner, or means of worship, or the society of worshippers he should join with in worship. Not but that a great abuse may be made of this doctrine of liberty of conscience in the worship of God. I know that many are ready to justify every thing in their own conduct from this doctrine, and I do not suppose that men's pretence of conscience is always to be regarded, when made use of to justify their changing the society of worshippers they unite with, or the means of their worship, or indeed the kind or manner of their worship. Men may make this pretence at times under such circumstances, that they may, obviously, be worthy of no credit in what they pretend. It may be manifest from the nature and circumstances of the case, and their own manner of behavior, that it is not conscience, but petulancy, and malice, and willfulness, and obstinacy, that influence them. And, therefore, it seems to me evident that when such pleas are made, those that are especially concerned with them as persons that are peculiarly obliged to take care of their souls, have no other way to do, but to consider the nature and circumstances of the case, and from thence to judge whether the case be such as will admit of such a plea, or whether the nature of things will admit of such a supposition, that the men act conscientiously in what they do, considering all things that appertain to the case.

And in this, I conceive many things are to be considered and laid together, as: the nature of that thing is the subject of controversy, or wherein they differ from others, or have changed their own practice; the degree in which it is disputable, or how it may be supposed liable to diversity of opinion, one way or the other, as to its agreeableness to the word of God, and as to the importance of it, with regard to men's salvation or the good of their souls; the degree of knowledge or ignorance of the persons, the advantages they had for information, or the disadvantages they have been under, and what has been in their circumstances that might mislead the judgment; the principles that have been instilled into them; the instructions they have received from those, of whose piety and wisdom they have had a high opinion, which might misguide the judgment of persons of real honesty, and sincerity, and tender conscience; the example of others; the diversity of opinion among ministers; the general state of things in the land; the character of the persons themselves; and the manner of their behavior in the particular affair in debate.

Now, Sir, with regard to those persons that have gone from you, to Windsor, however you may look upon their behavior herein as very disorderly, yet, if you suppose (the case being considered with all its circumstances) that there was any room for charity, that it might be through infirmity, ignorance, and error of judgment, so that they might be truly conscientious in it—that is, might really believe it to be their duty and what God required of them, to do as they have done—you would, I imagine, by no means think that they ought to be proceeded with, in the use of such means as are proper to be used with contumacious offenders, or those that are stubborn and obstinate in scandalous vice and willful wickedness; or that you would think it proper to proceed with persons, towards whom there is this room left for charity, that possibly they may be honest and truly conscientious, acting as persons afraid to offend God, so as to cut them off from the communion of the Lord, and cast them forth into the visible kingdom of Satan, to be as harlots and publicans.

Now, it may be well to examine, whether it can positively be determined, when all things are taken into consideration with respect to these persons who have absented themselves from your assembly, that it is not possible in their case, that this might really be their honest judgment, that it was their duty to do so, and that God required it of them, and that they should greatly expose the welfare of their own souls, in attending no other public worship but that in your congregation. I suppose these persons are not much versed in casuistical divinity.[2] They are of the common people, whose judgments, in all nations and ages, are exceedingly led and swayed. They are not very capable of viewing things in the extent of their consequences, and of estimating things in their true weight and importance. And you know, dear Sir, the state that things have been in, in the country. You know what opinions have lately prevailed, and have been maintained and propagated by those that have been lifted up to heaven in their reputation for piety and great knowledge in spiritual things, with a great part of the people of New England. I do not pretend to know what has influenced these people, in particu-

---

2. That is, divinity or theology that relates to the resolution of those situations where there is a conflict of duties.

lar; but I think, under these circumstances, it would
be no strange thing if great numbers of the common
people in the country, who are really conscientious
and concerned to be accepted with God and to take
the best course for the good of their souls, should
really think in their hearts that God requires them to
attend the ministry of those that are called New Light
Ministers and that it would be dangerous to their
souls, and what God approved not of, ordinarily to
attend the ministry of others; yea, I should think it
strange if it were otherwise.

It ought to be considered how public controversy,
and a great and general cry in matters of religion,
strongly influences the conduct of multitudes of
the common people, how it blinds their minds, and
wonderfully misleads their judgments. And the rules
of the gospel and the example of the apostles most
certainly require that great allowances be made in
such cases. And particularly the example of the
apostle Paul, with regard to great numbers of professing Christians, in the church of Corinth; who, in a
time of great and general confusion in that church,
through the evil instructions of teachers whom they
admired, who misled and blinded their judgments,
ran into many and great disorders in their worship,
and woeful schisms and divisions among themselves,
particularly with regard to ministers, and even with
regard to the apostle Paul himself, whom many of
them seem for a time to have forsaken to follow others
who set up themselves in opposition to him, though,
as he says, he had been their father who begat them

through the gospel.[3] Yet with how much gentleness does the apostle treat them, still acknowledging them as brethren; and though he required church censures to be used with regard to the incestuous person,[4] yet there is no intimation of the apostle taking any such course, with those that had been misled by these false teachers, or with any that had been guilty of these disorders, except with the false teachers themselves. But as soon as they are brought off from following these false apostles any longer, he embraces them without further ado, with all the love and tenderness of a father; burying all their censoriousness, and schisms, and disorders, at the Lord's Supper, as well as their ill treatment of him, the extraordinary messenger of Christ to them.

And, indeed, the apostle never so much as gave any direction for the suspension of any one member from the Lord's Supper on account of these disorders or from any other part of the public worship of God. But instead of this, [he] gives them directions how they shall go on to attend the Lord's Supper, and other parts of worship, in a better manner. And he himself, without suspension or interruption, goes on to call and treat them as beloved brethren, Christians, sanctified in Christ Jesus, called to be saints; and praises God in their behalf, for the grace that is given to them by Christ Jesus; and often and abundantly exhibits his charity towards them in innumerable expressions which I might mention. And nothing is more apparent than that he does not treat them

---

3. An allusion to 1 Corinthians 4:15.

4. See 1 Corinthians 5.

as persons with respect to whom there lies a bar in the way of others treating them with the charity that belongs to saints, and good and honest members of the Christian church, until the bar be removed by a church process. And, indeed, the insisting on a church process with every member that has behaved disorderly, in such a state of general confusion, is not a way to build up the church of God (which is the end of church discipline), but to pull it down. It will not be the way to cure a diseased member, but to bring a disease on the whole body.

...The objections that these persons may have had against ordinarily attending your meeting may be very trivial. But yet I suppose that, through infirmity, the case may be so with truly honest Christians, that trivial things may have great weight in their consciences, so as to have fast hold of them, until they are better enlightened. As in the former times of the country, it was with respect to the controversy between Presbyterians and Congregationalists. It was, as I have heard, in those days real matter of question with some, whether a Presbyterian, living and dying such, could be saved. Some Presbyterians that have lived with us, have desired baptism for their children, who yet lived in neglect of the ordinances of the Lord Jesus Christ, because of a difference in some trivial circumstances of the administration, from the method of the Church of Scotland.[5] This matter being discoursed of, it was

---

5. This is a reference to the fact that the Presbyterian Church of Scotland was accustomed to celebrate the Lord's Supper but four times a year, while Congregationalists had it more frequently. Edwards himself was in favor of "the administration of the Lord's

thought by Col. Stoddard in particular,[6] that their neglect ought to be borne with, and they ought to be looked upon as Christians, and their children received to baptism, because, however trivial the foundation of their scruples were, yet through ignorance they might be honest and conscientious in them.

...And if it be so that these persons, in some of their conversation and behavior, have manifested a contentious, forward spirit, at the time of their withdrawing from your church, I confess this gives greater ground of suspicion of the sincerity of their plea of conscience. Yet, as to this, I humbly conceive allowances must be made. It must be considered that it is possible that persons, in an affair of this nature, may, in the thing itself, be conscientious, and yet, in the course of the management of it, may be guilty of very corrupt mixtures of passion and every evil disposition, as indeed is commonly the case with men,

---

Supper every Lord's Day" (Letter to John Erskine, November 15, 1750 ["Memoirs," cxxiii]).

6. John Stoddard (1682-1748) was Edwards' uncle, one of his strongest supporters, and an influential figure in the affairs of Northampton. For details about Edwards' relationship with Col. Stoddard, one can look up the various pages referenced in the index entry in Marsden, 613.

See also Edwards' funeral sermon for him: *A Strong Rod Broken and Withered* (Boston, 1748), in Jonathan Edwards, *Sermons and Discourses 1743-1758*, ed. Wilson H. Kimnach, vol. 25 of *The Works of Jonathan Edwards* (New Haven/London: Yale University Press, 2006), 315-329. In this sermon Edwards states that Stoddard was "no inconsiderable divine: he was a wise casuist, as I know by the great help I have found from time to time, by his judgment and advice in cases of conscience, where I have consulted him" (*Sermons and Discourses 1743-1758*, ed. Kimnach, 325).

in long controversies of whatever nature, and even with conscientious men. And therefore it appears to me, that if persons in such a case are not obstinate, in what is amiss in them in this respect, and don't attempt to justify their forwardness and unchristian speeches, they notwithstanding may deserve credit, when they profess themselves conscientious in the affair in general.

Thus, dear Sir, I have freely communicated to you some of my thoughts, with regard to some of the concerns of this difficult day, which prove a trouble to you, not however with any aim at directing your conduct, but merely to comply with the request to which I have alluded. I am fully sensible, that I am not the pastor of the second church of Hartford. And I only desire you would impartially consider the reasons I have offered. Begging of Christ, our common Lord, that he would direct you in your theory and practice, to that which will be acceptable in his sight,

I remain, Rev. Sir, Your friend and brother,
Jonathan Edwards.

10

To William McCulloch[1]

Northampton, March 5, 1744

Rev. and dear Sir,

...It has been slanderously reported and printed concerning me that I have often said that the millennium was already begun, and that it began at

---

1. From "Memoirs," lxxviii-lxxxi, *passim*. William McCulloch (1691-1771) was the Church of Scotland minister of Cambuslang—at that time a rural parish a few miles to the southeast of Glasgow—and was instrumental in the inception of what is known as the Cambuslang revival. McCulloch was far from being an accomplished speaker. In the jargon then current, he was a yill- or ale-minister, a term that was used of ministers whose preaching was so dry that when their turn came to preach at the large outdoor communion gatherings then held once a year by the Scottish churches, many of the audience would leave to quench their thirst from nearby ale barrels provided for refreshment. Yet it was under McCulloch's preaching in mid-February, 1742, that, according to the English Congregationalist Philip Doddridge (1702-1751), around one hundred and thirty people, most of whom had sat under McCulloch's preaching for a number of years, "were awakened on a sudden to attend to it, as if it had been a new revelation brought down from heaven, and attested by as astonishing miracles as ever were wrought by Peter or Paul" (*Some Remarkable Passages in the Life of the Honourable Col. James Gardiner* §135 in *The Works of The Rev. P. Doddridge, D.D.* [Leeds, 1803], IV, 88).

Sharing a common desire for God-glorifying revival, McCulloch and Edwards were in regular correspondence from 1743 onwards. Ten of Edwards' letters to the Scottish pastor have been preserved. See Mitchell, "Jonathan Edwards's Scottish Connection," 229-230.

Northampton. A doctor of divinity in New England has ventured to publish this report to the world,[2] from a single person, who is concealed and kept behind the curtain. But the report is very diverse from what I have ever said. Indeed I have often said, as I say now, that I looked upon the late wonderful revivals of religion as forerunners of those glorious times so often prophesied of in the Scripture, and that this was the first dawning of that light, and beginning of that work, which, in the progress and issue of it, would at last bring on the church's latter-day glory.[3] But there are many that know that I have from time to time added, that there would probably be many sore conflicts and terrible convulsions, and many changes, revivings, and intermissions, and returns of dark clouds, and threatening appearances, before this work shall have subdued the world, and Christ's kingdom shall be everywhere established and settled in peace, which will be the lengthening of the millennium or day of the church's peace, rejoicing, and triumph on earth, so often spoken of.

---

2. Edwards is referring to Charles Chauncy (1705-1787), the co-pastor of Boston's prestigious First Church, one of the most influential ministers of his day and an ardent foe of revival. After Edwards' death, he embraced Unitarianism.

3. Edwards was a post-millennialist. His eschatological thought is well explored by C. C. Goen, "Jonathan Edwards: A New Departure in Eschatology," *Church History*, 28 (1959): 25-40; John F. Wilson, "History, Redemption, and the Millennium" in Nathan Hatch and Harry S. Stout, eds., *Jonathan Edwards and the American Experience* (New York/Oxford: Oxford University Press, 1988), 131-141; Stephen J. Stein, "Eschatology" in Sang Hyun Lee, ed., *The Princeton Companion to Jonathan Edwards* (Princeton/Oxford: Princeton University Press, 2005), 226-242.

...I believe that, before the church of God shall have obtained the conquest, and the visible kingdom of Satan on earth shall receive its overthrow, and Christ's kingdom of grace be everywhere established on its ruins, there shall be a great and mighty struggle between the kingdom of Christ and the kingdom of Satan, attended with the greatest and most extensive convulsions and commotion, that ever were upon the face of the earth, wherein doubtless many particular Christians will suffer, and perhaps some parts of the church.

But that the enemies of the church of God should ever gain such advantages against her any more, as they have done in times past, that the victory should ever any more be on their side, or that it shall ever be given to the beast again to make war with the saints, and to prevail against them, and overcome them (as in Revelation 13:7 and 11:7, and Daniel 7:21) to such a degree as has been heretofore, is otherwise than I hope. Though in this I would be far from setting up my own judgment, in opposition to others, who are more skilled in the prophecies of Scripture than I am. I think that what has mainly induced many divines to be of that opinion is what is said in Revelation 11 concerning the slaying of the witnesses, verses 7-8, "And when they shall have finished their testimony, the beast, that ascendeth out of the bottomless pit, shall make war against them, and shall overcome them, and kill them. And their dead bodies shall lie in the street of the great city," etc.

The event here spoken of seems evidently to be that wherein the enemies of the church gain the greatest advantage against her that ever they have, and have the greatest conquest of her that ever they obtained, and bring the church nearest to a total extinction.... But are we to expect this, dear Sir, that Satan will ever find means to bring things to pass, that after all the increase of light that has been in the world, since the Reformation, there shall be a return of a more dark time than in the depth of the darkness of popery, before the Reformation, when the church of God shall be nearer to a total extinction, and have less of visibility, all true religion and light be more blotted out of the memories of mankind, Satan's kingdom of darkness be more firmly established, all monuments of true religion be more abolished, and that the state of the world should be such, that it should appear further from any hope of a revival of true religion than it ever has done. Is this conceivable or possible, as the state of things now is all over the world, even among papists themselves, without a miracle, a greater than any power short of divine can effect, without a long tract of time, gradually to bring it to pass, to introduce the grossest ignorance and extinguish all memory and monuments of truth, which was the case in that great extinction of true religion that was before the Reformation?

...But in these things, dear Sir, I am by no means dogmatical. I do but humbly offer my thoughts on what you suggested in your letter, submitting them to your censure. 'Tis pity that we should expect such a terrible devastation of the church before her last and most glorious deliverance, if there be no such thing to be expected. It may be a temptation to some of the people of God, the less earnestly to wish and pray for the near approach of the church's glorious day, and the less to rejoice in the signs of its approach.

But, let us go on what scheme we will, it is most apparent from the Scriptures, that there are mighty strugglings to be expected before her great victory. And there may be many lesser strugglings before that last, and greatest, and universal conflict. Experience seems to show that the church of God, according to God's method of dealing with her, needs a great deal gradually to prepare her for that prosperity and glory that he has promised her on earth, as the growth of the earth, after winter, needs gradually to be prepared for the summer heat. I have known instances, wherein by the heat's coming on suddenly in the spring, without intermissions of cold to check the growth, the branches, many of them, by a too hasty growth, have afterwards died. And perhaps God may bring on a spiritual spring as he does the natural, with now and then a pleasant sun-shiny season, and then an interruption by clouds and stormy winds, till at length, by the sun more and more approaching, and the light increasing, the strength of the winter is broken. We are extremely apt to get out of the right way. A very great increase of comfort that is sudden, without time and experience, in many instances, has appeared to wound the soul, in some respects, though it seems to profit it in others. Sometimes, at the same time that the soul seems wonderfully delivered from those lusts, that are more carnal and earthly, there is an insensible increase of those that are more spiritual; as God told the children of Israel, that he would put out the former inhabitants of the land of Canaan, by little and little, and would not consume them at once, lest the beasts of the field should increase upon them.

We need much experience, to teach us the innumerable ways that we are liable to err, and to show us the evil and pernicious consequences of those errors. If it should please God, before many years, to grant another great revival of religion in New England, we should perhaps be much upon our guard against such errors as we have run into, and which have undone us this time, but yet might run insensibly into other errors that now we think not of.

...Dear brother, asking your earnest prayers for me and for New England, I am your affectionate brother, and engaged friend and servant,

Jonathan Edwards.

11

To Joseph Bellamy[1]

Northampton, January 15, 1747

Dear Sir,

...As to the books you speak of: Mastricht is sometimes in one volume, a very large thick quarto, sometimes in two quarto volumes. I believe it could not be had new under 8 or 10 pounds. Turretin is in three volumes in quarto, and would probably be about the same price.[2] They are both excellent. Turretin is on polemical divinity, on the 5 points & all

---

1. From Stanley T. Williams, ed., "Memoranda and Documents: Six Letters of Jonathan Edwards to Joseph Bellamy," *The New England Quarterly*, 1 (1928): 228-232, *passim*.

2. Edwards is referring to Peter van Mastricht, *Theoretica-Practica Theologia* (New ed.; Utrecht, 1699) and François Turretin, *Institutio Theologiae Elencticae* (Geneva, 1679-1685).

Van Mastricht (1630-1706) was a Dutch theologian who was the professor of theology at Utrecht from 1677 onwards. His life and teaching are scarcely known today. On Mastricht's theology, see Richard A. Muller, *Post-Reformation Reformed Dogmatics* (2nd ed.; Grand Rapids: Baker, 2003), 4 vols., *passim;* Adriaan Cornelis Neele, *The Art of Living to God: A Study of Method and Piety in the Theoretico-Practica Theologia of Petrus van Mastricht (1630-1706)* (Pretoria: University of Pretoria, 2005).

It is noteworthy that little has been done to examine the theological influence of Mastricht on Edwards' thought. See, however, Amy Plantinga Pauw's discussion of Mastricht's influence on Edwards' Trinitarian theology: *"The Supreme Harmony of All": The Trinitarian Theology of Jonathan Edwards* (Grand Rapids/Cambridge, U.K.: Wil-

Peter van Mastricht (1630-1706)

other controversial points, & is much larger in these than Mastricht, & is better for one that desires only to be thoroughly versed in controversies. But take Mastricht for divinity in general, doctrine, practice & controversy, or as an universal system of divinity; & it is much better than Turretin or any other book in the world, excepting the Bible, in my opinion.

...I have been reading Whitby,[3] which has engaged me pretty thoroughly in the study of the Arminian controversy; and I have written considerably upon it in my private papers.... I have got so deep into this

---

liam B. Eerdmans Publ. Co., 2002), 27-28, 30, 36-37, 58-59, 61-64, 69, 74-75, 142, 156-157.

Tryon Edwards, one of Edwards' great-grandsons, notes that Edwards eventually sent a copy of Mastricht to Bellamy, which the latter used in the writing of his *True Religion Delineated* (1750) ("Memoir [of Joseph Bellamy]" in *The Works of Joseph Bellamy, D.D.* [Boston: Doctrinal Tract and Book Society, 1853], I, xiv, n.*).

Turretin (1623-1687), an important "seventeenth-century Swiss systematizer of Reformed theology" (Marsden, 318), taught theology in Geneva and was a zealous critic of Amyraldianism. For a brief overview of his life and teaching, see Harriet A. Harris, "Turretin, Francis" in Trevor A. Hart, ed., *The Dictionary of Historical Theology* (Carlisle, Cumbria/Waynesboro, Georgia: Paternoster Press/Grand Rapids/Cambridge, UK: William B. Eerdmans Publ. Co., 2000), 553-554.

3. Daniel Whitby (1638-1726) was a theologian with open Arminian tendencies who appears to have departed from biblical Trinitarianism in his final days. For a brief overview of his thinking, see Paul Ramsey, "Editor's Introduction" in his edition of Jonathan Edwards, *A careful and strict Enquiry into The modern prevailing Notions of...Freedom of Will*, vol. 1 of *The Works of Jonathan Edwards* (New Haven/London: Yale University Press, 1957), 81-82. Edwards refuted his implicit Arminianism in his *Freedom of the Will* (1754). On Edwards' conviction that Whitby was not a total Arminian, see his Letter to John Erskine, July 7, 1752 ("Memoirs," cxlv).

controversy, that I am not willing to dismiss it till I know the utmost of these matters.[4]

I have very lately received a packet from Scotland, with several copies of a memorial for the continuing and propagating an agreement for joint prayer for the general revival of religion;[5] three of which I here send

---

4. The result of these studies would be Edwards' *Freedom of the Will*. Numerous studies have appeared on this vital work. See especially, C. Samuel Storms, "Jonathan Edwards on the Freedom of the Will," *Trinity Journal*, N.S., 3 (1982), 131-169; *idem*, "The Will: Fettered Yet Free (*Freedom of the Will*)" in John Piper and Justin Taylor, eds., *A God Entranced Vision of All Things: The Legacy of Jonathan Edwards* (Wheaton, Illinois: Crossway Books, 2004), 201-220 (an annotated bibliography appears at the end of this article); and Allen C. Guelzo, "Freedom of the Will" in Lee, ed., *Princeton Companion to Jonathan Edwards*, 115-129. Stephen J. Nichols provides a popular overview of this work in *Jonathan Edwards: A Guided Tour of His Life and Thought* (Phillipsburg, New Jersey: P&R Publishing, 2001), 173-187.

5. This correspondence from Scotland informed Edwards about a prayer movement for revival which had been formed by a number of Scottish evangelical ministers, including a number of regular correspondents of Edwards—McCulloch, MacLaurin of the Ramshorn Church, Glasgow, James Robe, and John Erskine (1721-1803), then of Kirkintilloch. On Erskine, see below, page 95, n. 1.

These ministers and their congregations had agreed to spend a part of Saturday evening and Sunday morning each week, as well as the first Tuesday of February, May, August, and November, in prayer to God for "an abundant effusion of his Holy Spirit" so as to "revive true religion in all parts of Christendom, and to deliver all nations from their great and manifold spiritual calamities and miseries, and bless them with the unspeakable benefits of the kingdom of our glorious Redeemer, and fill the whole earth with his glory" (*Humble Attempt* in *Apocalyptic Writings*, ed. Stephen J. Stein, vol. 5 of *The Works of Jonathan Edwards* [New Haven/London: Yale University Press, 1977], 321). This "concert of prayer" ran for an initial two years, and then was renewed for a further seven.

When Edwards was sent information regarding this concert of

A N

Humble Attempt

To promote

Explicit Agreement

A N D

Viſible U N I O N

Of God's People in

Extraordinary Prayer

For the REVIVAL of *Religion* and the Advancement of *Chriſt's Kingdom* on Earth,
purſuant to Scripture-Promiſes and Prophecies concerning the *laſt Time*.

By *Jonathan Edwards*, A. M.
Miniſter of the Goſpel at *Northampton*.

With a PREFACE by ſeveral Miniſters.

B O S T O N, NEW-ENGLAND :
Printed for D. HENCHMAN in *Cornhil*. 1747.

you, desiring you to dispose of two[6] of 'em where they will be most serviceable. For my part, I heartily wish it was fallen in with by all Christians from the rising to the setting sun.

---

prayer, he lost no time in seeking to implement a similar concert in the New England colonies. He encouraged his own congregation to get involved, and also communicated the concept of such a prayer union to neighboring ministers whom he felt would be receptive to the idea. Although the idea initially met with a poor response, Edwards was not to be put off. In a sermon given in February, 1747, on Zechariah 8:20-22, he sought to demonstrate how the text supported his call for a union of praying Christians. Within the year a revised and greatly expanded version of this sermon was ready for publication as the *An Humble Attempt to Promote Explicit Agreement and Visible Union of God's People in Extraordinary Prayer, For the Revival of Religion and the Advancement of Christ's Kingdom on Earth, pursuant to Scripture-Promises and Prophecies concerning the Last Time*, usually known simply as the *Humble Attempt*.

6. For the reading "two," see *Letters and Personal Writings*, 217.

12

To William McCulloch[1]

Northampton, January 21, 1747

Rev. and dear brother,

The time seems long to me since I have received a letter from you. I have had two letters from each of my other correspondents in Scotland since I have had any from you. Our correspondence has been to me very pleasant, and I am very loath it should fail.

…It appears to me, that God's late dealings, both with Great Britain and the American plantations, if they be duly considered, as they are in themselves and circumstances, afford just reason to hope that a day is approaching for the peculiar triumphs of divine mercy and sovereign grace, over all the unworthiness, and most aggravated provocations of men. If it be considered what God's past dealings have been with England and Scotland for two centuries past, what obligations he has laid those nations under, and particularly the mercies bestowed more lately. And [if] we then well consider the kind, manner, and degree, of the provocations and wickedness of those nations, and yet that God so spares them, and has of late so remarkably delivered them, when so exposed to deserved destruction. And if it be also considered what God's dealings have been with this land, on its

1. From "Memoirs," lxxxvi-lxxxvii.

first settlement, and from its beginning hitherto, and how long we have been revolting and growing worse, and what great mercy he has lately granted us, on the late remarkable striving of his Spirit with us, and how his Spirit has been treated, his mercy and grace despised, and bitterly opposed, how greatly we have backslidden, what a degree of stupidity we are sunk into, and how full the land has been of such kinds of wickedness, as have approached so near to the unpardonable sin against the Holy Ghost, and how obstinate we are still in our wickedness, without the least appearances of repentance or reformation. And [if] it be then considered how God has of late made his arm bare, in almost miraculous dispensations of his providence, in our behalf, to succeed us against our enemies, and defend us from them.[2] I say, if these things be considered, it appears evident to me, not only that God's mercies are infinitely above the mercies of men, but also that he has, in these things, gone quite out of the usual course of his providence and manner of dealings with his professing people. And I confess it, it gives me great hope that God's appointed time is approaching, for the triumphs and displays of his infinite, sovereign grace, beyond all that ever has been before, from the beginning of the world.

At least I think there is much in these things, considered together with other remarkable things God has lately done, to encourage and animate God's

---

2. A reference to military victories obtained by British and American forces against the French in Canada during King George's War (1744-1748). For Edwards' thoughts about this war, see Marsden, 310-319.

people unitedly to cry to God, that he would appear for the bringing on those glorious effects of his mercy, so often foretold to be in the latter days; and particularly to continue that concert for prayer, set on foot in Scotland, and which it is now proposed to continue seven years longer.[3]

My wife and children join with me in respectful, cordial salutations to you and yours. That we may be remembered in your prayers, is the request, dear Sir, of your affectionate brother,

Jonathan Edwards.

---

3. On the concert of prayer, see above, pages 85-86.

Sarah Edwards (1710-1758)

13

---•◦•---

To Sarah Edwards[1]

Northampton, June 22, 1748

My Dear Companion,

I wrote you a few lines the last Sabbath day by
Ensign Dwight,[2] which I hope you will receive. By
this I would inform you that Betty[3] seems really to be
on the mending hand; I can't but think she [is] truly
better, both as her health and her sores, since she has
been at Mrs. Phelps'.[4] The first two or three days,

---

1. From Clarence H. Faust and Thomas H. Johnson, *Jonathan
Edwards: Representative Selections* (New York: American Book Company, 1935), 384.

For Sarah Edwards (1710-1758), see the references in Murray
and Marsden. On the marriage of Jonathan and Sarah, see especially
the recent study by Doreen Moore, *Good Christians, Good Husbands?
Leaving a Legacy in Marriage & Ministry* (Fearn, Ross-shire: Christian
Focus Publications, 2004), 96-127. See also Elisabeth D. Dodds,
*Marriage To a Difficult Man. The Uncommon Union of Jonathan & Sarah
Edwards* (1971 ed.; repr. Laurel, Mississippi: Audubon Press, 2004);
Noël Piper, "Sarah Edwards: Jonathan's Home and Haven" in John
Piper and Justin Taylor, eds., *A God Entranced Vision of All Things:
The Legacy of Jonathan Edwards* (Wheaton, Illinois: Crossway Books,
2004), 55-78. See also above, pages 8-12.

2. Timothy Dwight, Jr. See above, pages 19-21.

3. Elizabeth Edwards (1747-1762). For another reference to
Elizabeth's ill-health, see below, pages 133-134.

4. Miriam Phelps (*c.* 1711-1787) was a neighbor who seems to
have taken the baby Elizabeth while Sarah was away. See *Letters and
Personal Writings*, 247; Faust and Johnson, *Jonathan Edwards*, 429.

before she was well acquainted, she was very unquiet; but now more quiet than she used to be at home.

This is lecture-day morning, and your two eldest daughters[5] went to bed last night, both sick, and rose beat out, and having the headache. We got Hannah Root[6] to help them yesterday in the afternoon, and expect her again today. How Sarah [and] Esther do today I can't tell, for they are not up. We have been without you as long as we know how to be; but yet are willing you should obey the calls of providence with regard to Col. Stoddard.[7]

If you have money to spare, and it isn't too late, I should be glad if you would buy us some cheese in Boston, and [send it] with other things if it can be [sent] safely.

Give my humble service to Mr. Bromfield[8] and Madam[9] and proper salutation to other friends.

I am your most affectionate companion,
Jonathan Edwards.

---

5. Sarah Edwards (see above, pages 13-14) and Esther Edwards. On Esther, see above, pages 14-17. Esther was the third daughter. The second was Jerusha, who had died four months before this letter was written.

6. Hannah Root (born *c.* 1731), a resident of Northampton, possibly a servant who worked occasionally for Jonathan and Sarah. See *Letters and Personal Writings*, 824.

7. On John Stoddard, see above, page 74, n. 6. He died unexpectedly in Boston on June 15, 1748. Providentially, Sarah was there and able to care for him. See Marsden, 343.

8. Edward Bromfield (1695-1756), a Boston merchant, who frequently hosted Edwards and his family in Boston. See *Letters and Personal Writings*, 808.

9. Abigail Coney Bromfield (*Letters and Personal Writings*, 247).

14

-----•)•-----

To John Erskine[1]

Northampton, August 31, 1748

Rev. & dear Sir,

I this summer received your kind letter of February 9, 1748, with your most acceptable present of Taylor on *Original Sin*, and his *Key to the Apostolic Writings*, with his *Paraphrase on the Epistle to the Romans*;[2] together with your *Sermons* and *Answer to*

---

1. From "Memoirs," xcv. When Edwards wrote this letter to John Erskine, the latter was ministering in Kirkintilloch, Scotland. Later he became the minister of the historic church of Old Greyfriars, Edinburgh. Erskine was responsible for getting a number of Edwards' works published in Scotland. He has been well described as "the paradigm of Scottish evangelical missionary interest through the last half of the eighteenth century" (J.A. De Jong, *As the Waters Cover the Sea. Millennial Expectations in the Rise of Anglo-American Missions 1640-1810* [Kampen, The Netherlands: J.H. Kok N.V., 1970], 166). On his correspondence with Edwards, see Mitchell, "Jonathan Edwards's Scottish Connection," 232-239. For a brief overview of his life and work, see Ned C. Landsman, "Erskine, John," *Oxford Dictionary of National Biography*, eds. H. C. G. Matthew and Brian Harrison (Oxford: Oxford University Press, 2004), 18:558-560.

2. John Taylor (1694-1761) was a noted Hebraist and strident critic of classical Calvinism. Although he believed in the infallibility of the Scriptures, Taylor saw no foundation for the doctrine of original sin in Scripture. Edwards' critique of his position can be found in his *The Great Christian Doctrine of Original Sin Defended* (1757).

The gravestone of Jerusha Edwards (1730-1748)
in the Northampton cemetery, whose death
is mentioned in this letter to John Erskine.

(Photograph: Ron Baines)

Dr. Campbell.[3] I had your Sermons before, sent either
by you or Mr. MacLaurin.

I am exceedingly glad of those two books of
Taylor's. I had before borrowed and read Taylor on
Original Sin; but am very glad to have one of my own;
if you had not sent it, I intended to have sought opportunity to buy it. The other book, his *Paraphrase*...I had
not heard of. If I had I should not have been easy till
I had seen it and been possessed of it. These books,
if I should live, may probably be of great use to me.
Such kindness from you was unexpected. I hoped to
receive a letter from you, which alone I should have
received as a special favor.

I have for the present been diverted from the design
I hinted to you, of publishing something against some
of the Arminian tenets, by something else that divine
Providence unexpectedly laid in my way, and seemed
to render unavoidable, viz. publishing Mr. Brainerd's
Life,[4] of which the enclosed paper of proposals give
some account.

---

3. *The People of God considered as All Righteous* (Edinburgh, 1745)
and *The Law of Nature* (Edinburgh, 1745).

4. *An Account of the Life Of the late Reverend Mr. David Brainerd*
(1749) has never been out of print since its publication. The memoir of David Brainerd is undoubtedly one of the most important of
Edwards' works.

For studies of this work and its impact, see Joseph Conforti,
"Jonathan Edwards's Most Popular Work: 'The Life of David Brainerd' and Nineteenth-Century Evangelical Culture," *Church History*, 54
(1985): 188-201; David B. Calhoun, "David Brainerd: 'A Constant
Stream,'" *Presbyterion*, 13 (1987): 44-50; [Gray Brady], "Books in
History: Edwards on *David Brainerd*," *The Evangelical Library Bulletin*
97 (Winter 1996): 6-8; Andrew F. Walls, "Missions and Historical

It might be of particular advantage to me, here in this remote part of the world, to be better informed what books there are that are published on the other side of the Atlantic, and especially if there be any thing that comes out that is very remarkable. I have seen many notable things that have been written in this country against the truth, but nothing very notable on our side of the controversies of the present day, at least of the Arminian controversy. You would much oblige me, if you would inform me what are the best books that have lately been written in defense of Calvinism.

...It has pleased God, since I wrote my last to you, sorely to afflict this family, by taking away by death, the last February, my second daughter, in the eighteenth year of her age; a very pleasant and useful member of this family, and one that was esteemed the flower of the family.[5] Herein we have a great loss;

Memory: Jonathan Edwards and David Brainerd" in Kling and Sweeney, eds., *Jonathan Edwards at Home and Abroad*, 248-265.

5. Seventeen-year old Jerusha Edwards (1730-1748) had nursed David Brainerd (1718-1747) through the entire time of his illness in the home of Edwards. She died of a fever on February 14, a Sunday. Edwards was grief-stricken. The shock may have been in part because she had been ill for only five days before her death. As he tells Erskine, what comforted him and his family was that there had been "remarkable appearances of piety" in her life from childhood. In a letter written to his close friend Joseph Bellamy on April 4, 1748, Edwards had mentioned that David Brainerd regarded Jerusha "as a saint,...a very eminent saint" (Williams, ed., "Six Letters of Jonathan Edwards to Joseph Bellamy," 236).

Jerusha's nursing of Brainerd and their being buried side by side have given rise to all kinds of romanticizing about their being engaged to one another. Stanley T. Williams, for example, speaks of their

but the remembrance of the remarkable appearances of piety in her, from her childhood, in life, and also at her death, are very comfortable to us, and give us great reason to mingle thanksgiving with our mourning. I desire your prayers, dear Sir, that God would make up our great loss to us in himself.

"betrothal and love" ("Six Letters of Jonathan Edwards to Joseph Bellamy," 234). There is no solid evidence, however, that there was such a betrothal between David and Jerusha.

15

To John Erskine[1]

Rev. and dear Sir,

A little while ago I wrote a letter to you, wherein I acknowledged the receipt of your letter, and the books that came with it, viz. Taylor on *Original Sin* and on the *Romans*, with your sermons and *Answer to Mr. Campbell*, for which most acceptable presents I would most heartily and renewedly thank you.

…As to my writing against Arminianism, I have hitherto been remarkably hindered, so that probably it will be a considerable time before I shall have anything ready for the press, but do intend, God allowing and assisting, to prosecute that design. And I desire your prayers for the divine assistance in it. The books you sent me will be a great help to me. I would on no account have been without them.

…I condole with you and Mrs. Erskine, on the loss of your noble and excellent father, which is doubtless a great loss to the church of God.[2] But the glorious King of Zion, who was dead, is alive and lives for evermore, and can raise up others in exalted stations to favor Zion, and seems to be so doing at this

---

1. From "Memoirs," c-ci.

2. Erskine's father-in-law who died in 1748 was George Mackay, the third Baron Reay. See *Letters and Personal Writings*, 265, n. 4.

day, by things you give an account of in your letter. I have been the subject of an afflictive dispensation of late, tending to teach me how to sympathize with the afflicted, which I think I mentioned in my last letter to you, viz. the death of my second daughter, the last February.

Please to present my most affectionate and respectful salutations to your dear consort. That I and mine may be remembered in your and her prayers, is the request of your affectionate and obliged friend and brother,

Jonathan Edwards.

16

To John Erskine[1]

Northampton, May 20, 1749

Rev. and dear Sir,

The day before yesterday, I received your letter of February 14, with a packet, containing the pamphlets you mention in your letter, for which I am greatly obliged to you. I have not yet had opportunity to read these books, but promise myself much entertainment by them, from the occasions on which they were written, and the subject they are upon. The last letter I received from you before this, was dated April 6, 1748, so that I suppose the two letters you say you wrote to me, since those which I acknowledge the receipt of, have miscarried, which I much regret, as I much value what comes from your hand.

...I shall send orders to Boston, that one of my books on Mr. Brainerd's *Life* may be sent to you with this letter, if any of them are ready, as I hope they are, or will be very speedily.

I have nothing very comfortable to inform you of concerning the present state of religion in this place. A very great difficulty has arisen between my people, relating to qualifications for communion at the Lord's Table. My honored grandfather Stoddard,[2] my prede-

---

1. From "Memoirs," civ-cv.

2. Solomon Stoddard (1643-1729), Edwards' maternal grand-

cessor in the ministry over this church, strenuously maintained the Lord's Supper to be a converting ordinance, and urged all to come, who were not of scandalous life, though they knew themselves to be unconverted. I formerly conformed to his practice. But I have had difficulties with respect to it, which

---

father, was a powerful preacher and pastor of the Congregational Church in Northampton from 1669 till his death in 1729. Edwards co-pastored with him for two years from 1727 to 1729. Stoddard was sometimes described by his theological opponents as a "congregational Pope" (Marsden, 32).

By 1690 Stoddard had come to the view that the Lord's Table is "a converting ordinance." As he said in a sermon that he preached that year on Galatians 3:11, this text clearly indicates that the "Lord's Supper is appointed...for the begetting of grace as well as for the strengthening of grace." This innovation, known today as Stoddardeanism, was fiercely attacked by a number of New England Congregationalists, including the Puritan poet Edward Taylor (c. 1645-1729), pastor in Westfield, Massachusetts. Stoddard's able defense of his views, though, convinced many in western Massachusetts and Stoddardeanism became the official position of the Northampton congregation.

Now, the conviction that this practice was thoroughly unscriptural had been deepening in Edwards' mind for quite some time before he openly declared in December of 1748 that a person must profess to be regenerate before he or she would be allowed to come to the Lord's Table. In taking this position Edwards found himself opposed by most of his congregation, as he details in this letter.

On Stoddard, see especially Patricia J. Tracy, "Stoddard, Solomon," *American National Biography* (New York/Oxford: Oxford University Press, 1999), 26:822-823; Paul R. Lucas, " 'The Death of the Prophet Lamented': The Legacy of Solomon Stoddard" in Stephen J. Stein, ed., *Jonathan Edwards's Writings: Text, Context, Interpretation* (Bloomington/Indianapolis: Indiana University Press, 1996), 69-84; Mark Garrett Longaker, "Puritan Sermon Method and Church Government: Solomon Stoddard's Rhetorical Legacy," *The New England Quarterly*, 79 (2006): 439-460.

AN
HUMBLE INQUIRY

INTO THE

RULES OF THE WORD OF GOD,

CONCERNING THE

QUALIFICATIONS

REQUISITE TO A

COMPLETE STANDING AND FULL COMMUNION

IN THE

VISIBLE CHRISTIAN CHURCH.

By the Late JONATHAN EDWARDS, A. M.
THEN PASTOR OF THE FIRST CHURCH IN NORTHAMPTON;
AFTERWARDS PRESIDENT OF THE COLLEGE OF
NEW JERSEY.

WITH AN APPENDIX BY MR. FOXCROFT.

EDITION SECOND.

BEHOLD NOW I HAVE OPENED MY MOUTH:—MY WORDS SHALL
BE OF THE UPRIGHTNESS OF MY HEART.   JOB XXXIII. 2. 3.

EDINBURGH:

PRINTED FOR WILLIAM COKE, LEITH.

Anno 1790.

have been long increasing, till I dared no longer to proceed in the former way; which has occasioned great uneasiness among my people, and has filled all the country with noise, which has obliged me to write something on the subject, which is now in the press.[3] I know not but this affair will issue in a separation between me and my people. I desire your prayers, that God would guide me in every step of this affair. My wife joins with me in respectful salutations to you and your consort.

I am, dear Sir, your obliged and affectionate brother and servant,

Jonathan Edwards.

---

3. This is Edwards' *An Humble Inquiry into the Rules of the Word of God concerning the Qualifications Requisite to a Complete Standing and Full Communion in the Visible Christian Church* (1749). A critical edition of this text can be found in David D. Hall, ed., *Jonathan Edwards: Ecclesiastical Writings*, vol. 12 of *The Works of Jonathan Edwards* (New Haven/London: Yale University Press, 1994), 165-348. For an overview of this work, see Nichols, *Jonathan Edwards*, 125-137.

For discussions of the communion controversy, see Murray, 311-349; Marsden, 341-374; David D. Hall, "Editor's Introduction" to his ed., *Jonathan Edwards: Ecclesiastical Writings*, 17-86; Mark Dever, "How Jonathan Edwards Got Fired, and Why It's Important for Us Today" in John Piper and Justin Taylor, eds., *A God Entranced Vision of All Things: The Legacy of Jonathan Edwards* (Wheaton, Illinois: Crossway Books, 2004), 129-144.

17

To Mary Edwards[1]

Northampton, July 26, 1749

My dear child,

You may well think it is natural for a parent to be concerned for a child at so great a distance, so far out of view, and so far out of the reach of communication;[2] where, if you should be taken with any dangerous sickness, that should issue in death, you might probably be in your grave before we could hear of your danger. But yet, my greatest concern is not for your health, or temporal welfare, but for the good of your soul. Though you are at so great a distance from us, yet God is everywhere. You are much out of the reach of our care, but you are every moment in his hands. We have not the comfort of seeing you, but he sees you. His eye is always upon you. And if you may but live sensibly near to God, and have his gracious presence, it is no matter if you are far distant from us. I had rather you should remain hundreds of miles distant from us, and have God near to you by his Spirit, than to have you always with us, and live at a distance from God.

---

1. From "Memoirs," cix. Mary Edwards was Jonathan and Sarah's fourth daughter. See above, pages 17-19.

2. Mary was in Portsmouth, New Hampshire. See Marsden, 355-356.

And if the next news we should hear of you, should be of your death, though that would be very melancholy; yet, if at the same time we should receive such intelligence concerning you, as should give us the best grounds to hope, that you had died in the Lord, how much more comfortable would this be, though we should have no opportunity to see you, or to take our leave of you in your sickness, than if we should be with you during all its progress, and have much opportunity to attend upon you, and converse and pray with you, and take an affectionate leave of you, and after all have reason to apprehend that you died without the grace and favor of God! It is comfortable to have the presence of earthly friends, especially in sickness, and on a deathbed. But the great thing is to have God our friend, and to be united to Christ, who can never die any more, and from whom our own death cannot separate us.

My desire and daily prayer is that you may, if it may consist with the holy will of God, meet with God where you are, and have much of his divine influences on your heart, wherever you may be; and that, in God's due time, you may be returned to us again, in all respects under the smiles of heaven, and especially, in prosperous circumstances in your soul, and that you may find us all alive and well.... May God fit us all for his will!

I hope that you will maintain a strict and constant watch over yourself, against all temptations, that you do not forsake and forget God, and particularly, that you do not grow slack in secret religion. Retire often from this vain world, from all its bubbles and empty shadows, and vain amusements, and converse with

God alone; and seek effectually for that divine grace and comfort, the least drop of which is worth more than all the riches, gaiety, pleasures, and entertainments of the whole world.

…We are all, through the divine goodness, in a tolerable state of health. The ferment in the town runs very high concerning my opinion about the sacrament; but I am no more able to foretell the issue than when I last saw you. But the whole family has indeed much to put us in mind, and make us sensible, of our dependence on the care and kindness of God, and of the vanity of all human dependences; and we are very loudly called upon to seek his face, to trust in him, and walk closely with him. Commending you to the care and special favor of our heavenly Father, I am

Your very affectionate father,

Jonathan Edwards.

Your mother and all the family give their love to you.

18

──⊷ ⊷(0)⊷ ⊷──

To Joseph Bellamy[1]

Northampton, December 6, 1749

My dear Friend,

…As for the present state of things here with regard to our controversy,[2] 'tis not very easy for me to give you an idea of it, without writing a sheet or two of paper. But in brief, things are in great confusion. The tumult is vastly greater than when you was here, and is rising higher & higher continually. The people have got their resentments up to a great height towards you since you have been gone, and you are spoken of by 'em with great indignation & contempt.…

I have been openly reproached in church meetings, as apparently regarding my own temporal interest more than the honour of Christ & the good of the Church. As to the affair of a public dispute, it was quickly at an end after you went from hence. The people at their next parish meeting rejected it, as what would tend to make parties among us. They seem to be determined that the arguments for my opinion shall never be publicly heard, if it be possible to prevent it.…[3]

---

1. From Williams, ed., "Six Letters of Jonathan Edwards to Joseph Bellamy," 237-240, *passim.*

2. The communion controversy in Northampton. See above, pages 103-106.

3. Here, Edwards refers to his desire to have a public forum

You may easily be sensible dear Sir, that 'tis a time of great trial with me, and that I stand in continual need of the divine presence & merciful conduct in such a state of things as this. I need God's counsel in every step I take & every word I speak; so all that I do & say is watched by the multitude around me with the utmost strictness & with eyes of the greatest uncharitableness & severity and let me do or say what I will, my words & actions are represented in dark colours, and the state of things is come to that, that they seem to think it greatly concerns 'em to blacken me & represent me in odious colours to the world, to justify their own conduct. They seem to be sensible that now their character can't stand unless it be on the ruin of mine. They have publicly voted that they will have no more sacraments; & they have no way to justify themselves in that, but to represent me as very bad. I therefore desire dear Sir, your fervent prayers to God. If He be for me, who can be against me? If He be with me, I need not fear ten thousands of the people. But I know myself unworthy of his presence & help, yet would humbly trust in his infinite Grace & all sufficiency.

My Love to your spouse. I am your brother & near friend,

Jonathan Edwards.

---

in which he could present his views to the congregation. See Marsden, 357.

19

To John Erskine[1]

Northampton, July 5, 1750

Rev. and Dear Brother

...Your letter written in December, I received a little while ago. I have greatly regretted the want of opportunity to answer you till now; but such have been my extraordinary circumstances, the multitude of distracting troubles and hurries that I have been involved in (which I cannot easily represent to you) that I have had no leisure. I have been very uneasy in neglecting to write to my correspondents in Scotland; and about two months ago I set myself to the business, but was soon broken off; and have not been able to return to it again till now. And now, my dear Sir, I thank you for your letters and presents. The books you sent me were entertaining to me, and some of them will be of advantage to me, if God should give me opportunity to prosecute the studies I had begun on the Arminian controversy. There were various things pleasing to me in Glas's *Notes*,[2] tending to give

---

1. From "Memoirs," cxviii-cxxi, *passim*.

2. John Glas, *Notes on Scripture Texts* (Edinburgh, 1747-1760). John Glas (1695-1773) was the minister of the Church of Scotland work in Tealing, Scotland, and a man of considerable erudition. Gradually he came to the conviction that Christ's kingdom is one that is completely spiritual and as such independent of both state control and support. A church of some seventy believers was formed

A

FAREWEL-SERMON

Preached at the first Precinct in

NORTHAMPTON,

After the People's publick Rejection of their Minister, and re-
nouncing their Relation to Him as Pastor of the Church there,

On *June* 22. 1750.

Occasion'd by Difference of Sentiments,
concerning the requisite Qualifications
of Members of the Church, in compleat
Standing.

By *Jonathan Edwards,* A. M.

Acts xx. 18. *Ye know, from the first Day that I came into* Asia,
after what Manner I have been with you, at all Seasons.
ver. 20.   *And how I kept back nothing that was profitable unto you ;
but have shewed you, and have taught you publickly, and from House
to House.*
ver. 26, 27.   *Wherefore I take you to Record this Day, that I am pure
from the Blood of all Men : For I have not shunned to declare unto
you all the Counsel of God.*
Gal. iv. 15, 16.   *Where is then the Blessedness ye spake of ? For I
bear you Record, that if it had been possible, ye would have plucked
out your own Eyes, and have given them to me.   Am I therefore become your Enemy, because I tell you the Truth ?*

BOSTON:

Printed and Sold by S. Kneeland over against the Prison in *Queen-
Street.* 1751.

some new light into the sense of Scripture. He seems
to be a man of ability, though I cannot fall in with all
his singularities.

...The absurdities of the Moravians are not very
surprising to me.[3] I have seen here in America so

---

in the parish of Tealing, and over the next couple of decades Glasite
congregations could be found in Dundee, Perth, Edinburgh, and
booming textile centers such as Paisley and Dunkeld. Although the
Glasites were never numerous, Glas' views exercised a wide sphere
of influence, especially through the travels of his son-in-law, Robert
Sandeman (1718-1771), throughout the British Isles and America.

The Glasites or Sandemanians—they were called by both names—
adopted such practices as foot-washing, the love feast, and holy
kissing (from which, in New England at least, they were derisively
called "Kissites"). They insisted on the use of lots to determine God's
will, and on unanimity in all church decisions. The insistence of Glas
and Sandeman on such "trivia of church order" set them apart from
the mainstream of eighteenth-century Evangelicalism. More signifi-
cantly, Glas' and Sandeman's followers also distinguished themselves
from other eighteenth-century Evangelicals by a predominantly
intellectualist view of faith. They became known for their cardinal
theological tenet that saving faith is "bare belief of the bare truth."

For further discussion, see Derek B. Murray, "The Influence of
John Glas," *Records of the Scottish Church History Society*, 22 (1984):
45-56; *idem*, "An Eighteenth-Century Baptismal Controversy in
Scotland" in Stanley E. Porter and Anthony R. Cross, eds., *Baptism,
the New Testament and the Church. Historical and Contemporary Studies
in Honour of R.E.O. White* (Sheffield Academic Press, 1999), 419-429;
Thomas J. South, "The Response of Andrew Fuller to the Sandema-
nian View of Saving Faith" (unpublished Th.D. thesis, Mid-America
Baptist Theological Seminary, 1993), 47-57.

3. Certain elements of Moravian spirituality were a source of
controversy during the eighteenth century. Moravian stress on the
wounds of Christ—their "blood and wounds" theology—the use of
the term "Mother" for the Holy Spirit, their doctrine of "stillness" in
the process of conversion (simply waiting upon God for conversion)
and their view of marriage as a sacrament were offensive to other

much of the tendency and issue of such kind of
notions, and such sort of religion, as are in vogue
among them, and among others in many respects
like them, that I expect no other than that sin, folly,
absurdity, and things to the last degree reproachful to
Christianity will forever be the consequence of such
things. It seems to me that enough and enough of
this kind has lately appeared, greatly to awaken the
attention of Christian divines, and make them suspect

Evangelicals. Nevertheless, under the leadership of Nicolaus von
Zinzendorf (1700-1760), eighteenth-century Moravian missionaries
went out literally to the four corners of the earth: to the West Indies
in 1732, to Greenland in 1733, to Lapland and Georgia in 1734, to
Surinam in 1735, to South Africa in 1737, to Algeria in 1739, to Sri
Lanka and Romania in 1740, and to Persia in 1747. By Zinzendorf's
death in 1760 no fewer than 226 missionaries had been sent out by
this tiny community. Not surprisingly, they became a stimulus to the
late eighteenth-century missionary movement.

Looking back on this amazing outburst of missionary energy,
William Wilberforce (1759-1833), the great English Evangelical poli-
tician and social reformer, could say of the Moravians at the end of
the eighteenth century: "They are a body who have perhaps excelled
all mankind in solid and unequivocal proofs of the love of Christ and
of ardent, active zeal in His service. It is a zeal tempered with prudence, softened with meekness and supported by a courage which no
danger can intimidate and a quiet certainty no hardship can exhaust"
(cited Colin A. Grant, "Europe's Moravians—A pioneer missionary
church," *Evangelical Missions Quarterly,* 12 [1976]: 221).

See Geoffrey Stead, "Moravian Spirituality and its Propagation in
West Yorkshire during the Eighteenth-Century Evangelical Revival,"
The Evangelical Quarterly, 71 (1999): 233-259; J.C.S. Mason, *The
Moravian Church and the Missionary Awakening in England, 1760-1800*
(Woodbridge, Suffolk: Boydell Press, 2001); Ian Randall, "A Mis-
sional Spirituality: Moravian Brethren and eighteenth-century English
evangelicalism" (unpublished paper, 2006). For Zinzendorf, see A.J.
Lewis, *Zinzendorf: The Ecumenical Pioneer* (London: SCM, 1962).

that the devil's devices in the various counterfeits of vital, experimental religion, have not been sufficiently attended to, and the exact distinctions between the saving operations of the Spirit of God and its false appearances not sufficiently observed.

There is something now in the press at Boston, largely handling the subject. I have had opportunity to read the manuscript, and, in my humble opinion, it has a tendency to give as much light in this matter, as any thing that ever I saw. It was written by Mr. Bellamy, minister of Bethlehem, in Connecticut,[4] the minister whom Mr. Brainerd[5] sometimes speaks of as his peculiarly dear and intimate friend (as possibly you may have observed in reading his *Life*). He was of about Mr. Brainerd's age, and it might have been well, if he had had more years over his head. But as he is one of the most intimate friends that I have in the world, and one that I have much acquaintance with, I can say this of him, that he is one of very great experience in religion, as to what has passed between God and his own soul; one of very good natural abilities, of closeness of thought, of extraordinary diligence in his studies, and earnest care exactly to know the truth in these matters. He has long applied his mind to the subject be has wrote upon and used all possible helps of conversation and reading. And though his style is not such as is like to please the polite world, yet if his youth, and the obscurity of his original, and the place that he lives in, etc., do not prevent his being much taken notice of, I am persuaded his book might serve

---

4. On Bellamy, see above, page 51, n. 1.

5. That is, David Brainerd.

to give the church of God considerable light as to the nature of true religion, and many important doctrines of Christianity.[6] From the knowledge I have of him, I am fully satisfied that his aim in this publication is not his own fame and reputation in the world, but the glory of God, and the advancement of the kingdom of his Redeemer.

…I am very glad to hear of what Mr. MacLaurin informs me of the encouragements likely to be given from Scotland to New Jersey College, a very hopeful society, and I believe what is done for that seminary is doing good in an eminent manner.

Mr. MacLaurin tells me of some prospect of your being removed to a congregation in Edinburgh, which I am pleased with, because I hope there you will act in a larger sphere, and will have more opportunity to exert the disposition that appears in you, to promote good public designs for Zion's prosperity.[7]

…I desire that such a time of awful changes, dark clouds, and great frowns of heaven on me and my people may be a time of serious consideration, thorough self-reflection and examination, and deep humiliation with me. I desire your fervent prayers for me, and for those who have heretofore been my people. I know not what will become of them. There seems to be the utmost danger, that the younger generation will be carried away with Arminianism as with a flood.

---

6. The book in question is *True Religion Delineated* (1750), for which Edwards wrote "a glowing preface" (Sweeney and Guelzo, eds., *New England Theology*, 73).

7. Erskine did not move until 1758 (*Letters and Personal Writings*, 813).

...An end is put for the present, by these troubles, to the studies I was before engaged in and my design of writing against Arminianism. I had made considerable preparation and was deeply engaged in the prosecution of this design, before I was rent off from it by these difficulties, and if ever God should give me opportunity, I would again resume that affair. But I am now, as it were, thrown upon the wide ocean of the world, and know not what will become of me and my numerous and chargeable family. Nor have I any particular door in view that I depend upon to be opened for my future serviceableness. Most places in New England that want a minister would not be forward to invite one with so chargeable a family, nor one so far advanced in years—being forty-six the fifth day of last October. I am fitted for no other business but study. I should make a poor hand at getting a living by any secular employment. We are in the hands of God, and I bless him. I am not anxious concerning his disposal of us. I hope I shall not distrust him, nor be unwilling to submit to his will. And I have cause of thankfulness that there seems also to be such a disposition in my family.

You are pleased, dear Sir, very kindly to ask me, whether I could sign the *Westminster Confession of Faith*, and submit to the Presbyterian form of church government, and to offer to use your influence to procure a call for me, to some congregation in Scotland. I should be very ungrateful, if I were not thankful for such kindness and friendship. As to my subscribing to the substance of the *Westminster Confession*, there would be no difficulty; and as to the Presbyterian government, I have long been perfectly out of conceit of our unsettled, independent, confused way of church government in this land. And the Presbyterian way has ever appeared to me most agreeable to the Word of God, and the reason and nature of things, though I cannot say that I think that the Presbyterian government of the Church of Scotland is so perfect that it cannot, in some respects, be mended. But as to my removing with my numerous family over the Atlantic, it is, I acknowledge, attended with many difficulties that I shrink at. Among other things, this is very considerable, that it would be on uncertainties, whether my gifts and administrations would suit any[8] congregation that should send for me without trial; and so great a thing as such a removal had need to be on some certainty as to that matter. If the expectations of a congregation were so great, and they were so confident of my qualifications, as to call me at a venture, having never seen nor heard me; their disappointment might possibly be so much the greater, and they the more uneasy after acquaintance and trial. My own country is not so dear to me, but that, if there were an evident prospect of being more serviceable to Zion's interests elsewhere, I could forsake it. And I think my wife is fully of this disposition.

…My wife and family join with me in most respectful and cordial salutations to you, and your consort; and we desire the prayers of you both for us, under our present circumstances. My youngest child but one[9] has long been in a very infirm, afflicted, and

---

8. Reading "any" (*Letters and Personal Writings*, 356) rather than "my" ("Memoirs," cxxi).

9. Jonathan Edwards, Jr. (1745-1801) lived to become an impor-

decaying state with the rickets, and some other disorders. I desire your prayers for it.

I am, dear Sir,

Your most affectionate and obliged friend and brother,

Jonathan Edwards.

---

tant theologian in his own. See Robert L. Ferm, *A Colonial Pastor. Jonathan Edwards the Younger: 1745-1801* (Grand Rapids: William B. Eerdmans Publ. Co., 1976).

Sir William Pepperrell (1696-1759)

(From James Truslow Adams, *Revolutionary New England 1691-1776* [Boston: The Atlantic Monthly Press, 1923], opposite p. 182)

20

To Lady Mary Pepperrell[1]

Stockbridge, November 28, 1751

Madam,

When I was at your house in Kittery the last
spring, among other instances of your kind and con-
descending treatment to me, was this, that, when I
had some conversation with Sir William concerning
Stockbridge and the affairs of the Indians, and he
generously offered me any assistance, in the business
of my mission here, which his acquaintance and correspondence in London enabled him to afford me,
and proposed my writing to him on our affairs; you
were also pleased to invite me to write to you at the
same time. If I should neglect to do as you then proposed, I should fail not only of discharging my duty,
but of doing myself a great honour. But as I am well
assured, even from the small acquaintance I had with
you, that a letter of mere compliments would not be
agreeable to a lady of your disposition and feelings,
especially under your present melancholy circum-

    1. From "Memoirs," cxxxix-cxl. Mary Pepperrell (b. 1689) was
the wife of Sir William Pepperrell (1696-1759), a merchant and an
ardent admirer of George Whitefield. He commanded the expedition
that took the fortress of Louisbourg in 1745. See Marsden, 310.

stances; so the writing of such a letter is very far from my intention or inclination.[2]

When I saw the evidences of your deep sorrow, under the awful frown of heaven in the death of your only son, it made an impression on my mind not easily forgotten. And when you spoke of my writing to you, I soon determined what should be the subject of my letter. It was that which appeared to me to be the most proper subject of contemplation for one in your circumstances; that, which I thought, above all others, would furnish you a proper and sufficient source of consolation, under your heavy affliction. And this was the Lord Jesus Christ, particularly the amiableness of his character, which renders him worthy that we should love him, and take him for our only portion, our rest, hope, and joy; and his great and unparalleled love towards us. And I have been of the same mind ever since; being determined, if God favoured me with an opportunity to write to your Ladyship, that those things should be the subject of my letter. For what other subject is so well calculated to prove a balm to the wounded spirit?

Let us then, dear Madam, contemplate the loveliness of our blessed Redeemer, which entitles him to our highest love, and, when clearly seen, leads us to find a sweet complacency and satisfaction of soul in him, of whatever else we are deprived. The Scriptures assure us that he, who came into the world in our nature and freely laid down his life for us, was truly possessed of all the fullness of the Godhead, of his

---

2. Edwards is writing a letter of consolation on the death of the Pepperrell's son.

infinite greatness, majesty, and glory, his infinite wisdom, purity, and holiness, his infinite righteousness and goodness. He is called "the brightness of God's glory, and the express image of his person."[3] He is the Image, the Expression, of infinite beauty, in the contemplation of which God the Father had all his unspeakable happiness from eternity. That eternal and unspeakable happiness of the Deity is represented as a kind of social happiness, in the society of the persons of the Trinity—Proverbs 8:30, "Then I was by him, as one brought up with him; I was daily his delight, rejoicing always before him." This glorious Person came down from heaven to be "the Light of the world,"[4] that by him the beauty of the Deity might shine forth, in the brightest and fullest manner, to the children of men.

Infinite Wisdom also has contrived that we should behold the glory of the Deity in the face of Jesus Christ,[5] to the greatest advantage, in such a manner as should be best adapted to the capacity of poor feeble man. In such a manner, too, as is best fitted to engage our attention, and allure our hearts, as well as to inspire us with the most perfect complacency and delight. For Christ having, by his incarnation, come down from his infinite exaltation above us, has become one of our kinsmen and brothers. And his glory shining upon us through his human nature, the manifestation is wonderfully adapted to the strength of the human vision, so that, though it appears in all

---

3. Hebrews 1:3.

4. John 8:12.

5. See 2 Corinthians 4:6.

its effulgence, it is yet attempered[6] to our sight. He is indeed possessed of infinite majesty to inspire us with reverence and adoration. Yet that majesty need not terrify us, for we behold it blended with humility, meekness, and sweet condescension. We may feel the most profound reverence and self-abasement, and yet our hearts be drawn forth sweetly and powerfully into an intimacy the most free, confidential, and delightful. The dread, so naturally inspired by his greatness, is dispelled by the contemplation of his gentleness and humility; while the familiarity, which might otherwise arise from the view of the loveliness of his character merely, is ever prevented by the consciousness of his infinite majesty and glory; and the sight of all his perfections united fills us with sweet surprise and humble confidence, with reverential love and delightful adoration.

This glory of Christ is properly, and in the highest sense, divine. He shines in all the brightness of glory that is inherent in the Deity. Such is the exceeding brightness of this Sun of righteousness, that, in comparison of it, the light of the natural sun is as darkness; and hence, when he shall appear in his glory, the brightness of the sun shall disappear, as the brightness of the little stars do when the sun rises. So says the prophet Isaiah, "Then the moon shall be confounded, and the sun shall be ashamed, when the Lord of hosts shall reign in Mount Zion, and before his ancients gloriously" (Isaiah 24:23). But, although his light is thus bright, and his beams go forth with infinite strength, yet, as they proceed

---

6. That is, suitably modified.

from the Lamb of God, and shine through his meek
and lowly human nature, they are supremely soft and
mild, and, instead of dazzling and overpowering our
feeble sight, like a smooth ointment or a gentle eye-
salve, are vivifying and healing. Thus on them, who
fear God's name, "the Sun of righteousness arises,
with healing in his beams" (Malachi 4:2). It is like the
light of the morning, a morning without clouds, as the
dew on the grass, under whose influence the souls of
his people are as the tender grass springing out of the
earth, by clear shining after rain. Thus are the beams
of his beauty and brightness fitted for the support and
reviving of the afflicted. He heals the broken in spirit
and bindeth up their wounds. When the spirits of his
people are cut down by the scythe, he comes down
upon them, in a sweet and heavenly influence, "like
rain on the mown grass, and like showers that water
the earth" (Psalm 72:6).

But especially are the beams of Christ's glory
infinitely softened and sweetened by his love to men,
the love that passeth knowledge.[7] The glory of his
person consists pre-eminently, in that infinite goodness and grace, of which he made so wonderful a
manifestation, in his love to us. The apostle John
tells us that "God is light" (1 John 1:5) and again,
that "God is love" (1 John 4:8) and the light of his
glory is an infinitely sweet light, because it is the
light of love. But especially does it appear so, in the
person of our Redeemer, who was infinitely the most
wonderful example of love that was ever witnessed.
All the perfections of the Deity have their highest

---

7. Cp. Philippians 4:7.

manifestation in the work of redemption, vastly more than in the work of creation. In other works, we see him indirectly. But here, we see the immediate glory of his face (2 Corinthians 3:18). In his other works, we behold him at a distance. But in this, we come near, and behold the infinite treasures of his heart (Ephesians 3:8-10).

It is a work of love *to us,* and a work of which *Christ* is the author. His loveliness and his love have both their greatest and most affecting manifestation in those sufferings, which he endured *for us* at his death. Therein, above all, appeared his holiness, his love to God, and his hatred of sin, in that, when he desired to save sinners, rather than that a sensible testimony should not be seen against sin, and the justice of God be vindicated, he chose to become "obedient unto death, even the death of the cross."[8] Thus, in the same act, he manifests, in the highest conceivable degree, his infinite hatred of sin and his infinite love to sinners. His holiness appeared like a fire, burning with infinite vehemence against sin. At the same time,... his love to sinners appeared like a sweet flame, burning with an infinite fervency of benevolence. It is the glory and beauty of his love to us, polluted sinners, that it is an infinitely pure love. And it is the peculiar sweetness and endearment of his holiness, that it has its most glorious manifestation in such an act of love to us. All the excellencies of Christ, both divine and human, have their highest manifestation in this wonderful act of his love to men—his offering up himself a sacrifice for us, under these extreme sufferings.

---

8. Philippians 2:8.

Herein have abounded toward us the riches of his grace, "in all wisdom and prudence" (Ephesians 1:8). Herein appears his perfect justice. Herein, too, was the great display of his humility, in being willing to descend so low for us. In his last sufferings appeared his obedience to God, his submission to his disposing will, his patience, and his meekness, when he went as a lamb to the slaughter, and opened not his mouth, but in a prayer that God would forgive his crucifiers. And how affecting this manifestation of his excellency and amiableness to our minds, when it chiefly shines forth in such an act of love to us. The love of Christ to men, in another way, sweetens and endears all his excellencies and virtues; as it has brought him in to so near a relation to us, as our friend, our elder brother, and our redeemer; and has brought us into an union so strict with him, that we are his friends, yea, "members of his body, of his flesh, and of his bones" (Ephesians 5:30).

We see then, dear Madam, how rich and how adequate is the provision, which God has made for our consolation, in all our afflictions, in giving us a Redeemer of such glory and such love, especially, when it is considered, what were the ends of this great manifestation of beauty and love in his death. He suffered that we might be delivered. His soul was exceeding sorrowful, even unto death, to take away the sting of sorrow, and to impart everlasting consolation. He was oppressed and afflicted, that we might be supported. He was overwhelmed in the darkness of death, that we might have the light of life. He was cast into the furnace of God's wrath, that we might drink of the rivers of his pleasures. His soul was overwhelmed with a flood of sorrow, that our hearts might be overwhelmed with a flood of eternal joy.

We may also well remember, in what circumstances our Redeemer now is. He was dead; but he is alive, and he lives for evermore. Death may deprive us of our friends here, but it cannot deprive us of this our best Friend. We have this best of friends, this mighty Redeemer, to go to, in all our afflictions, and he is not one who cannot be touched with the feeling of our infirmities. He has suffered far greater sorrows than we have ever suffered; and *if* we are actually united to him, the union can never be broken, but will continue when we die, and when heaven and earth are dissolved.

Therefore, in this we may be confident, though the earth be removed, in him we shall triumph with everlasting joy. Now, when storms and tempests arise, we may resort to him, who is a hiding-place from the storm, and a covert from the tempest. When we thirst, we may come to him, who is as rivers of water in a dry place. When we are weary, we may go to him, who is as the shadow of a great rock in a weary land. Having found him, who is as the apple-tree among the trees of the wood, we may sit under his shadow with great delight, and his fruit will be sweet to our taste. Christ said to his disciples, "In the world ye shall have tribulation; but in me ye shall have peace"![9] If we are united to him, we shall be like a tree planted by the waters and that spreadeth out its roots by the river, that shall not see when heat cometh, but its leaf shall ever be green, and it shall not be careful in the year

---

9. John 16:33. Edwards has reversed the order of the clauses.

of drought, neither shall it cease from yielding fruit.[10] He will now be our light in darkness; our morning-star, shining as the sure harbinger of approaching day. In a little time, he will arise on our souls, as the sun in his glory; and our sun shall no more go down, and there shall be no interposing cloud—no veil on his face, or on our hearts. But the Lord shall be our everlasting light, and our Redeemer our glory.

That this glorious Redeemer would manifest his glory and love to your mind, and apply what little I have said on this subject to your consolation in all your afflictions, and abundantly reward your kindness and generosity to me while I was at Kittery, is the fervent prayer, Madam, of

Your Ladyship's most obliged and affectionate friend, and most humble servant,

Jonathan Edwards.

---

10. Cp. Psalm 1:3.

21

To William McCulloch[1]

Stockbridge, November 24, 1752

Rev. and dear Sir,

I thank you for your letter of March 3, 1752, which I received this fall. I thank you for your friendly and instructive observations, on God's dealings with me and my family. Though God's dispensations towards me, have been attended with some distinguishing trials, yet the end of the Lord has been very gracious. He has ever manifested himself very pitiful and of tender mercy, in the midst of difficulties we have met with, in merciful circumstances with which they have been attended, and also in the event of them....

God has been very gracious to my family of late, when some of them have been visited with sore sickness. My wife has lately been very dangerously sick, so as to be brought to the very brink of the grave. She had very little expectation of life, but seemed to be assisted to an unweaned resignation to the divine will, and an unshaken peace and joy in God, in the expectation of a speedy departure. But God was pleased to preserve her, and mercifully to restore her to a pretty good state of health. My youngest daughter also,[2] who has been a very infirm child, was

---

1. From "Memoirs," cliii-cliv.

2. Elizabeth Edwards.

brought nigh unto death by a sore fit of sickness, and is now also restored to her former state. My daughter Parsons, my eldest daughter,[3] who with her husband has removed from Northampton and dwells in Stock-bridge, has also very lately been very sick, but is in a considerable measure restored. My daughter Esther's marriage with President Burr, of Newark, seems to be very much to the satisfaction of ministers and people in those parts, and also of our friends in Boston, and other parts of New England.[4]

As to the state of religion in America, I have but little to write that is comfortable; but there seems to be better appearances in some other colonies than in New England. When I was lately in New Jersey, in the time of the synod there, I was informed of some small movings and revivals in some places on Long-Island and New Jersey. I there had the comfort of a short interview with Mr. Davies of Virginia, and was much pleased with him and his conversation.[5] He

---

3. Sarah had married Elihu Parsons in the summer of 1750 (Marsden, 363).

4. On Esther, see above, pages 14-17.

5. Samuel Davies (1723-1761), though never a strong man physically, had a powerful ministry of awakening and revival in Virginia. A prodigious worker, he succeeded Edwards as the fourth President of the College of New Jersey, but died of pneumonia after only nineteen months in office. In the opinion of Mark Noll, had Davies survived he might have become the most notable American college president before the War of Independence ("Davies, Samuel," *American National Biography*, eds. John A. Garraty and Mark C. Carnes [New York/Oxford: Oxford University Press, 1999], 6:160).

For other studies of his life, see George William Pilcher, ed., *The Reverend Samuel Davies Abroad: The Diary of a Journey to England and Scotland, 1753-55* (Urbana/Chicago/London: University of Illinois

appears to be a man of very solid understanding, discreet in his behavior, and polished and gentlemanly in his manners, as well as fervent and zealous in religion…. Mr. Davies represented before the synod, the great necessities of the people in the back parts of Virginia, where multitudes were remarkably awakened and reformed several years ago, and ever since have been thirsting after the ordinances of God. The people are chiefly from Ireland, of Scotch extraction.

…My wife joins with me in most respectful salutations to you and yours. Desiring your prayers, that God would be with us in all our wanderings through the wilderness of this world,

I am, dear Sir,

Your most affectionate brother, in the labors of the gospel,

Jonathan Edwards.

Press, 1967); *idem, Samuel Davies: Apostle of Dissent in Colonial Virginia* (Knoxville: The University of Tennessee Press, 1971); Thomas Talbot Ellis, "Samuel Davies: Apostle of Virginia," *The Banner of Truth*, 235 (April 1983), 21-27; *idem,* "Samuel Davies: Characteristics of Life and Message," *The Banner of Truth*, 236 (May 1983): 10-18; Iain H. Murray, *Revival and Revivalism: The Making and Marring of American Evangelicalism 1750-1858* (Edinburgh: The Banner of Truth Trust, 1994), 3-31.

A nineteenth-century rendition of the house in which
Edwards and his family lived while in Stockbridge.

(From John Warner Barber, *Historical Collections*
[Worcester: Warren Lazell, 1844], 98)

22

To Timothy Edwards[1]

Stockbridge, April, 1753

My dear child,

Before you will receive this letter, the matter will doubtless be determined, as to your having the small-pox. You will either be sick with that distemper, or will be past danger of having it, from any infection taken in your voyage. But whether you are sick or well, like to die or like to live, I hope you are earnestly seeking your salvation. I am sure there is a great deal of reason it should be so, considering the warnings you have had in word and in providence. That which you met with, in your passage from New York to Newark, which was the occasion of your fever, was indeed a remarkable warning, a dispensation full of instruction, and a very loud call of God to you, to make haste, and not to delay in the great business of religion. If you now have that distemper, which you have been threatened with, you are separated from your earthly friends, as none of them can come to see you. And if you should die of it, you have already taken a final and everlasting leave of them while you are yet alive, so as not to have the comfort of their presence and immediate care, and never to

---

1. From "Memoirs," clvi-clvii. Timothy Edwards (1738-1813) was Jonathan and Sarah's eldest son.

see them again in the land of the living. And if you
have escaped that distemper, it is by a remarkable
providence that you are preserved. And your having
been so exposed to it, must certainly be a loud call of
God, not to trust in earthly friends or anything here
below. Young persons are very apt to trust in parents
and friends when they think of being on a death-bed.
But this providence remarkably teaches you the need
of a better Friend, and a better Parent, than earthly
parents are—One who is everywhere present, and
all sufficient, that cannot be kept off by infectious
distempers, who is able to save from death, or to
make happy in death, to save from eternal misery,
and to bestow eternal life. It is indeed comfortable,
when one is in great pain, and languishing under sore
sickness, to have the presence, and kind care, of near
and dear earthly friends. But this is a very small thing
in comparison of what it is to have the presence of a
heavenly Father and a compassionate and almighty
Redeemer. In God's favor is life, and his loving-kindness is better than life. Whether you are in sickness or
health, you infinitely need this.

But you must know, however great need you
stand in of it, you do not deserve it. Neither is God
the more obliged to bestow it upon you for your
standing in need of it, your earnest desiring of it,
your crying to him constantly for it from fear of
misery, and taking much pains. Till you have sav-
ingly believed in Christ, all your desires, and pains,
and prayers lay God under no obligation. And, if
they were ten thousand times as great as they are,
you must still know, that you would be in the hands
of a sovereign God, who "hath mercy on whom he

will have mercy."[2] Indeed, God often hears the poor miserable cries of sinful vile creatures, who have no manner of true regard to him in their hearts. For he is a God of infinite mercy, and he delights to show mercy for his Son's sake, who is worthy, though you are unworthy, who came to save the sinful and the miserable, yea, some of the chief of sinners.

Therefore, there is your only hope, and in him must be your refuge, who invites you to come to him, and says, "Him that cometh to me, I will in no wise cast out."[3] Whatever your circumstances are, it is your duty not to despair, but to hope in infinite mercy, through a Redeemer. For God makes it your duty to pray to him for mercy; which would not be your duty, if it was allowable for you to despair. We are expressly commanded to call upon God in the day of trouble, and when we are afflicted, then to pray.

But, if I hear that you have escaped—either that you have not been sick, or are restored—though I shall rejoice and have great cause of thankfulness, yet I shall be concerned for you. If your escape should be followed with carelessness and security, and forgetting the remarkable warning you have had, and God's great mercy in your deliverance, it would in some respects be more awful than sore sickness. It would be very provoking to God and would probably issue in an increasing hardness of heart. And, it may be, divine vengeance may soon overtake you. I have known various instances of persons being remarkably warned in providence by being brought into very dan-

2. Romans 9:18.

3. John 6:37.

gerous circumstances, and escaping, and afterwards death has soon followed in another way. I earnestly desire that God would make you wise to salvation, and that he would be merciful and gracious to you in every respect, according as he knows your circumstances require. And this is the daily prayer of

Your affectionate and tender father,

Jonathan Edwards.

23

Letter to Edward Wigglesworth[1]

Stockbridge, February 11, 1757

Rev. and dear Sir:

I can't assign any particular acquaintance as my warrant for troubling you with these lines; not being one of them that have been favored with opportunities for such an advantage. I only write as a subject and friend of the same Lord, and a follower and fellow-disciple of the same Jesus. A regard to his interests has made me uneasy as ever since I read Dr. Mayhew's late book, some time the last year, and saw that marginal note of his, wherein he ridicules the doctrine of the Trinity.[2]

---

1. From Vergilius Ferm, *Puritan Sage: Collected Writings of Jonathan Edwards* (New York: Library Publishers, 1953), 639-640. The manuscript which Ferm copied this letter from was in the possession of Congregational Library Association, but has since been lost. It is also printed in Joseph S. Clark, *A Historical Sketch of the Congregational Churches in Massachusetts from 1620-1858* (Boston, 1858).

Edward Wigglesworth (*c.* 1693-1765) was, at the time of this letter, the first Hollis Professor of Divinity at Harvard. He was among those who had opposed the ministry of George Whitefield in the 1740s, but was, nevertheless, committed to Calvinism. See *Letters and Personal Writings*, 697-698.

2. Jonathan Mayhew (1720-1766), the pastor of Boston's West Church, had rejected the biblical doctrine of the Trinity in favor of Unitarianism in 1755. He argued that the defenders of classical

And my uneasiness was increased after I had
wrote to Mr. Foxcroft upon it,[3] and fully expressed
my sentiments to him concerning the call of God to
ministers that way, or others whose business it was to
teach the doctrines of Christianity, to appear publicly
on this occasion in defence of this doctrine. And he,
in reply, informed me that the same affair had been
proposed and considered at the board of overseers,
and in the issue nothing concluded to be done. Very
lately Mr. Emlyn's book[4] has fallen into my hands,
published in New England by one that calls himself a
layman, who, in his dedication to the ministers of the

Trinitarianism were guilty of innovation! See Pauw, *"The Supreme
Harmony of All,"* 25. On Mayhew, see Marsden, 433-436.

3. Thomas Foxcroft (1697-1769), a Boston minister, was Edwards'
literary agent. For a biographical study of Foxcroft, see Ronald A.
Basco, "Introduction" to *The Sermons of Thomas Foxcroft of Boston*
(Delmar, New York: Scholars' Facsimiles and Reprints, 1982), 7-20.
Foxcroft had Charles Chauncy for his co-pastor. As Basco notes, it
was a "curious" arrangement since Foxcroft was an ardent Calvinist,
and Chauncy increasingly Arminian in his sympathies during his
time as Foxcroft's partner in ministry. Also Foxcroft was firmly on
Edwards' side in the debates about the legitimacy of the Great Awakening while Chauncy was Edwards' fiercest critic. He also wrote a
commendatory preface to Edwards' *Humble Inquiry into the Rules of the
Word of God concerning the Qualifications Requisite to a Complete Standing
and Full Communion in the Visible Christian Church.*

The obituary that ran in the *Massachusetts Gazette* after his death
described Foxcroft as "a strict Calvinist;...he was no Trimmer, but
steadily and uniformly adhered to the Calvinist principles, which he
took to be the true Scripture ones; making them the chief subjects of
his pulpit discourses" (cited Basco, "Introduction," 11).

4. Thomas Emlyn, *An Humble Inquiry into the Scripture-Account of
Jesus Christ* (1702). Emlyn was the first Unitarian minister in England.

country, gives them an open and bold (though a very subtle and artful) challenge to answer that book and defend the proper deity of Christ, if they can. Since I have read this book I am abundantly confirmed that my opinion, signified to Mr. Foxcroft, was right, and that the call of God that someone should appear in open defence of this doctrine, is very loud and plain; and that an universal neglect of it in the churches of New England on this occasion, will be imputed by the Head of the church, whose glory is so struck at, as a lukewarmness that will be very displeasing.

Though I live so much at a distance, yet I know so much of the state of the country that I am persuaded it will be of very bad consequence. This piece, by many, will be looked upon as invincible. It will be concluded that those who maintain the divinity of Christ are afraid to engage, being conscious that they are unable to defend their cause, and the adversary will triumph, and that cause will more and more prevail.

Now, Sir, I humbly conceive that you, above all others in the land, are called to engage in this cause. You are set for the instruction of our youth in divinity in the principal seminary of learning, and it will be among them especially that these pernicious principles will be like to gain ground. Something from you will be more regarded and attended to than [from] any other person.

I have heard say that your health is not firm,[5] which may possibly be an objection with you against engaging in a laborious controversy, which, if once

---

5. Wigglesworth did decline to write in defense of the Trinity. On Edwards' own Trinitarian thought, see Pauw, *"The Supreme Harmony*

begun, may possibly be drawn out to a great length,
and probably spending your time in controversy may
be much against your inclination. But yet you doubtless will allow that the case may be so, that Christians
may be evidently called, in adverse providences, to
engage in very irksome and laborious services and to
run considerable ventures in the cause of their Lord,
trusting in him for strength and support, as men, in
a just war for their king, in many cases doubt not of
their being called to great fatigues and to very great
ventures even of life itself. And shall all stand by at
such a day as this, under the testimonies of God's
anger for our corruptions, which are already so great,
and see the cause of Christ trampled on and the chief
dignity and glory of the King of Zion directly and
boldly struck at, with a challenge to others to defend it
if they can, and be silent, every one excusing himself
from the difficulty and fatigue of a spiritual warfare?
I live one side, far out of the way. I know not what
the view of the ministers of the country is. I can only
judge what the case requires. I think Zion calls for
help. I speak as one of her sons. If nothing can be
done, I dread the consequences. I entreat you, Sir, for
Christ's sake, not lightly to refuse what I have proposed and requested, and forgive the freedom which
has been used by,

Honored Sir, with great esteem and respect,

Your son and servant,

Jonathan Edwards.

---

of All" and *idem*, "The Trinity" in Lee, *Princeton Companion to Jonathan Edwards*, 44-58.

24

To the Trustees of the College of New Jersey at Princeton[1]

Stockbridge, October 19, 1757

Rev. and Hon. Gentlemen,

I was not a little surprised, on receiving the unexpected notice, of your having made choice of me, to succeed the late President Burr, as the Head of Nassau Hall. I am much in doubt, whether I am called to undertake the business, which you have done me the unmerited honour to choose me for. If some regard may be had to my outward comfort, I might mention the many inconveniences, and great detriment, which may be sustained, by my removing, with my numerous family, so far from all the estate I have in the world, (without any prospect of disposing of it, under

---

1. From "Memoirs," clxxiv-clxxv. Nassau Hall was the main building of the College of New Jersey, which came to be called Princeton. Aaron Burr, Sr., who had been the second President of the College, had died earlier in the year. Burr was a minister who was deeply respected by Edwards and was married to Edwards' third daughter Esther (on Esther, see above, pages 14-17). Burr also served as the pastor of the Presbyterian church in Newark, New Jersey, where the school was initially located. On Burr's leadership of the school, see Thomas Jefferson Wertenbaker, *Princeton 1746-1896* (Princeton, New Jersey: Princeton University Press, 1946), 25-42. Wertenbaker notes that to "Aaron Burr, more than to any other man, Princeton is indebted for its foundation" (42).

Nassau Hall and the President's House,
the College of New Jersey

(From Varnum Lansing Collins, *Princeton* [New York:
Oxford University Press, 1914], opposite p. 39.)

present circumstances, but with great loss), now when we have scarcely got over the trouble and damage sustained by our removal from Northampton, and have but just begun to have our affairs in a comfortable situation, for a subsistence in this place; and the expense I must immediately be at, to put myself into circumstances, tolerably comporting with the needful support of the honours of the office I am invited to, which will not well consist with my ability.

But this is not my main objection. The chief difficulties in my mind, in the way of accepting this important and arduous office, are these two. First, my own defects, unfitting me for such an undertaking, many of which are generally known, beside others, of which my own heart is conscious. I have a constitution, in many respects peculiarly unhappy, attended with flaccid solids, vapid, sizy[2] and scarce fluids, and a low tide of spirits; often occasioning a kind of childish weakness and contemptibleness of speech, presence, and demeanor, with a disagreeable dulness and stiffness, much unfitting me for conversation, but more especially for the government of a college. This makes me shrink at the thoughts of taking upon me, in the decline of life, such a new and great business, attended with such a multiplicity of cares, and requiring such a degree of activity, alertness, and spirit of government, especially as succeeding one so remarkably well qualified in these respects, giving occasion to everyone to remark the wide difference. I am also deficient in some parts of learning, particularly in

---

2. That is, thick and viscous. "Sizy" was commonly used in the eighteenth century with reference to the blood.

algebra, and the higher parts of mathematics, and in the Greek Classics, my Greek learning having been chiefly in the New Testament. The other thing is this, that my engaging in this business will not well consist with those views, and that course of employ in my study, which have long engaged and swallowed up my mind, and been the chief entertainment and delight of my life. And here, honoured Sirs (emboldened, by the testimony I have now received of your unmerited esteem, to rely on your candour,) I will with freedom open myself to you.

My method of study, from my first beginning the work of the ministry, has been very much by writing, applying myself, in this way, to improve every important hint; pursuing the clue to my utmost, when anything in reading, meditation, or conversation, has been suggested to my mind, that seemed to promise light, in any weighty point; thus penning what appeared to me my best thoughts, on innumerable subjects, for my own benefit. The longer I prosecuted my studies, in this method, the more habitual it became, and the more pleasant and profitable I found it. The farther I travelled in this way, the more and wider the field opened, which has occasioned my laying out many things in my mind, to do in this manner, if God should spare my life, which my heart hath been much upon, particularly many things against most of the prevailing errors of the present day, which I cannot with patience see maintained, to the utter subverting of the gospel of Christ, with so high a hand, and so long contained a triumph, with so little control, when it appears so evident to me, that there is truly no foundation for any of this glorying and insult. I have already published something on one of the main points in dispute between the Arminians and Calvinists,[3] and have it in view, God willing, as I have already signified to the public, in like manner to consider all the other controverted points, and have done much towards a preparation for it.

But beside these, I have had on my mind and heart, which I long ago began, not with any view to publication, a great work, which I call a *History of the Work of Redemption*, a body of divinity in an entire new method, being thrown into the form of a history; considering the affair of Christian Theology, as the whole of it, in each part, stands in reference to the great work of redemption by Jesus Christ, which I suppose to be, of all others, the grand design of God, and the *summum* and *ultimum* of all the divine operations and degrees; particularly considering all parts of the grand scheme, in their historical order. The order of their existence, or their being brought forth to view, in the course of divine dispensations, or the wonderful series of successive acts and events; beginning from eternity, and descending from thence to the great work and successive dispensations of the infinitely wise God, in time, considering the chief events coming to pass in the church of God, and revolutions in the world of mankind, affecting the state of the church and the affair of redemption, which we have an account of in history or prophecy; till at last, we come to the general resurrection, last judgement, and consummation of all things, when it shall be said, *It is done. I am Alpha*

---

3. *A careful and strict Enquiry into The modern prevailing Notions of ...Freedom of Will* (1754).

and Omega, the Beginning and the End. Concluding my work, with the consideration of that perfect state of things, which shall be finally settled to last for eternity. This history will be carried on with regard to all three worlds, heaven, earth and hell; considering the connected, successive events and alterations in each, so far as the Scriptures give any light; introducing all parts of divinity in that order which is most scriptural and most natural; a method which appears to me the most beautiful and entertaining, wherein every divine doctrine will appear to the greatest advantage, in the brightest light, in the most striking manner, showing the admirable contexture and harmony of the whole.

I have also, for my own profit and entertainment, done much towards another great work, which I call the *Harmony of the Old and New Testament,* in three parts. The first, considering the Prophecies of the Messiah, his redemption and kingdom; the evidences of their references to the Messiah, etc., comparing them all one with another, demonstrating their agreement, true scope, and sense; also considering all the various particulars wherein those prophecies have their exact fulfilment; showing the universal, precise, and admirable correspondence between predictions and events. The second part, considering the Types of the Old Testament, showing the evidence of their being intended as representations of the great things of the gospel of Christ; and the agreement of the type with the antitype. The third and great part, considering the Harmony of the Old and New Testament, as to doctrine and precept. In the course of this work, I find there will be occasion for an explanation of a very great part of the holy Scriptures, which may, in such a view, be explained in a method, which to me seems the most entertaining and profitable, best tending to lead the mind to a view of the true spirit, design, life and soul of the Scriptures, as well as their proper use and improvement. I have also many other things in hand, in some of which I have made great progress, which I will not trouble you with an account of. Some of these things, if divine providence favour, I should be willing to attempt a publication of. So far as I myself am able to judge of what talents I have, for benefitting my fellow creatures by word, I think I can write better than I can speak.

My heart is so much in these studies that I cannot find it in my heart to be willing to put myself into an incapacity to pursue them any more in the future part of my life, to such a degree as I must, if I undertake to go through the same course of employ in the office of President that Mr. Burr did, instructing in all the languages and taking the whole care of the instruction of one of the classes, in all parts of learning, besides his other labours.

If I should see light to determine me to accept the place offered me, I should be willing to take upon me the work of a President, so far as it consists in the general inspection of the whole society; and to be subservient to the school, as to their order and methods of study and instruction, assisting, myself, in the immediate instruction in the arts and sciences—as discretion should direct, and occasion serve, and the state of things require—especially of the senior class; and added to all, should be willing to do the whole work of a professor of divinity, in public and private lectures, proposing questions to be answered, and some to be discussed in writing and free conversation, in meetings of graduates, and others, appointed in proper seasons, for these ends. It would be now out of my way, to spend time, in a constant teaching the languages, unless it be the Hebrew tongue, which I should be willing to improve myself in, by instructing others.

On the whole, I am much at a loss with respect to the way of duty in this important affair. I am in doubt, whether, if I should engage in it, I should not do what both you and I would be sorry for afterwards. Nevertheless, I think the greatness of the affair, and the regard due to so worthy and venerable a body as that of the trustees of Nassau Hall, requires my taking the matter into serious consideration. And unless you should appear to be discouraged by the things which I have now represented, as to any farther expectation from me, I shall proceed to ask advice of such as I esteem most wise, friendly and faithful, if, after the mind of the Commissioners in Boston is known, it appears that they consent to leave me at liberty, with respect to the business they have employed me in here.[4]

---

4. The Massachusetts Commissioners for the Propagation of the Gospel among the Indians in New England oversaw the Stockbridge mission.

25

To Esther Burr[1]

Stockbridge, November 20, 1757

Dear daughter,

I thank you for your most comfortable letter, but more especially would I thank God that has granted you such things to write. How good & kind is your heavenly Father! How do the bowels of his tender love and compassion appear while he is correcting you by so great a shake of his head! Indeed, he is a faithful God. He will remember his covenant forever and never will fail them that trust in him. But don't be surprised, or think some strange thing has happened to you, if after this light, clouds of darkness should return. Perpetual sunshine is not usual in this world, even to God's true saints. But I hope, if God should hide his face in some respect, even this will be in faithfulness to you, to purify you, & fit you for yet further & better light.

As to removing to Princeton, to take on me the office of President I have agreed with the Church here to refer it to a council of ministers, to sit here December 21, to determine whether it be my duty.... What the council will do, I can't tell. I shall endeavor

---

1. From Ferm, *Puritan Sage*, 617-618. Edwards wrote this letter to his daughter Esther after the death of her spouse, Aaron Burr, Sr.

as fairly and justly as possible to lay the matter before 'em with every material circumstance.

...As to Lucy's coming home, her mother will greatly need her, especially if we remove in the spring. But yet, whether your circumstances don't much more loudly call for her continuance there, must be left with you & her. She must judge whether she can come consistently with her health & comfort at such a season of the year. If she come, let her buy me a staff, & ask advice, & get a good one, or none.

...If you think of selling Harry your mother desires you not to sell him, without letting her know it.[2]

...We all unite in love to you, Lucy[3] & your children. Your Mother is very willing to leave Lucy's coming away wholly to you & her.

I am your most tender & affectionate Father
                        Jonathan Edwards.

---

2. Here Edwards is shown to be a man of his time. While condemning the slave trade, he did not disapprove of owning slaves. On this inconsistency in Edwards, see Kenneth P. Minkema, "Jonathan Edwards's Defense of Slavery," *The Massachusetts Historical Review*, 4 (2002): 23-59; Sherard Burns, "Trusting the Theology of a Slave Owner" in Piper and Taylor, eds., *God Entranced Vision*, 145-171. His abolitionist followers, the so-called New Divinity, were more consistent in this matter. See Charles E. Hambrick-Stowe, "All Things Were New and Astonishing: Edwardsian Piety, the New Divinity, and Race" in Kling and Sweeney, eds., *Jonathan Edwards at Home and Abroad*, 121-136.

3. Lucy Edwards (1736-1786) was the fifth of the Edwards children.

26

To Lucy Edwards[1]

Dear Lucy,

It seems to me to be the will of God that I must shortly leave you. Therefore give my kindest love to my dear wife, and tell her that the uncommon union, which has so long subsisted between us has been of such a nature, as I trust is spiritual, and therefore will continue forever.[2]

And I hope she will be supported under so great a trial, and submit cheerfully to the will of God. And as to my children, you are now like to be left fatherless, which I hope will be an inducement to you all to seek a Father who will never fail you.

---

1. From "Memoirs," clxxviii. Technically speaking this is not a letter. These were words taken down at the death-bed of Edwards and never mailed. Nor did Edwards intend them to be a letter. Yet, insofar as they were written down in an epistolary form by those who were there immediately after they were spoken, they seem to serve well as a final "letter" from the hand of Edwards.

2. The phrase "uncommon union" has long been taken as a perspective from which to view the marriage of Jonathan and Sarah. As Marsden notes, "Edwards always chose his words carefully, and 'uncommon union' was an expression of the deepest affection, coming from someone for whom the highest relations in the universe were unions of affections among persons. Most important for Jonathan, the union was spiritual and hence eternal" (494).

Jonathan Edwards' grave in Princeton Cemetery.

And as to my funeral, I would have it to be like Mr. Burr's;[3] and any additional sum of money that might be expected to be laid out that way, I would have it disposed to charitable uses.

3. Aaron Burr had given instructions that his funeral be marked by a lack of ostentation and expense, and that "the sum which must be expended at a fashionable funeral, above the necessary cost of a decent one, should be given to the poor out of his estate" ("Memoirs," clxxviii, n.†).

27

Sarah Edwards to Esther Burr[1]

Stockbridge, April 3, 1758

My very dear child,

What shall I say? A holy and good God has covered us with a dark cloud. O that we may kiss the rod, and lay our hands on our mouths! The Lord has done it. He has made me adore his goodness that we had him so long. But my God lives, and he has my heart. O what a legacy my husband, and your father, has left us! We are all given to God; and there I am, and love to be.

Your ever affectionate mother,

Sarah Edwards.

---

1. From "Memoirs," clxxix. Esther never saw this letter for she died four days after her mother wrote this letter to her ("Memoirs," clxxix). See Marsden, 495.

28

Susannah Edwards to Esther Burr[1]

My dear sister,   Stockbridge, April 3, 1758

My mother wrote this[2] with a great deal of pain in her neck, which disabled her from writing any more. She thought you would be glad of these few lines from her own hand.

O, sister, how many calls have we, one upon the back of another? O, I beg your prayers, that we, who are young in this family, may be awakened and excited to call more earnestly on God, that he would be our Father, and Friend forever.

My father took leave of all his people and family as affectionately as if he knew he should not come again. On the Sabbath afternoon he preached from these words, "We have no continuing city, therefore let us seek one to come."[3] The chapter that he read was Acts the 20th. O, how proper. What could he have done more? When he had got out of doors he turned about, "I commit you to God," said he. I doubt not but God will take a fatherly care of us, if we do not forget him.

I am your affectionate sister,

                    Susannah Edwards.

---

1. From "Memoirs," clxxix. Susannah Edwards (1740-1802) was in her eighteenth year when she wrote this poignant letter.

2. A reference to the previous letter.

3. See Hebrews 13:14.

APPENDIX

Jonathan Edwards' Last Will, and the Inventory of His Estate[1]

In the name of God Amen, the fourteenth day of March 1753.

I Jonathan Edwards of Stockbridge, in the Province of the Massachusetts Bay in New-England, being in my usual state of health of body, and in the perfect exercise of my understanding & memory, through the goodness of God; but considering the frailty and mortality of mankind, and having much in the infirmity of my constitution to put me in mind of death, and make me sensible of the great uncertainty of my life, do make and ordain this my Last Will and Testament.

And first of all, I give and commend my soul into the hands of God that gave it, and to the Lord Jesus Christ its glorious, all-sufficient, faithful, & chosen Redeemer, relying alone on the free and infinite mercy & grace of God through his worthiness & mediation, for its eternal salvation. And my body I commend to the earth, to be committed to the dust in decent Christian burial, at the discretion of my Executrix hereafter named, hoping, through the grace, faithfulness, and almighty power of my everlasting

1. From "Jonathan Edwards' Last Will, and the Inventory of His Estate," *The Bibliotheca Sacra*, 33 (1876): 439-442.

Redeemer, to receive the same again, at the last day, made like unto his glorious body.

...I give to such of my sons as shall be brought up to learning (if any of them shall be so brought up) my whole library[2] (excepting such part as is hereafter mentioned, as given to my Executrix) to be given into their possession, as soon as they have taken their first degree.

...I give to my beloved wife (whom I hereby constitute make and ordain the sole Executrix of this my last Will and Testament) all my manuscripts, and as many of my printed books as comes to ten pounds in lawful money of this Province, such as she shall choose: and to her I give no more of my library, in case one or more of my sons are brought up to learning, & take a degree at college. But in case none of

---

2. According to the inventory taken of Edwards' library after his death, it consisted of the following books and manuscripts ("Jonathan Edwards' Last Will, and the Inventory of His Estate," 446):

Of Folios 38 Vols.	£ 28	3	0
Quartos 34 Vols.	7	11	9
Octavos 99 Vols.	26	16	6
Duodecimos 130 Vols.	8	15	3
Books published by the owner lately deceased, 25 Vols.	4	16	7
Pamphlets 536	4	13	0

Manuscripts

Folio 15 Vols. }			
Quartos 15 Vols. }	6	0	0
Sermons 1074 Vols. }			

them should be brought up to learning, then I will that all my library should be her's. Also I give to her, my said Executrix (with the above-said limitations respecting my library) my whole estate, real & personal, both what is now in my possession, and also the portion of my father's estate which shall fall to me or my heirs, to be hers, her heirs & assigns forever, she paying out of it the fore-mentioned legacies[3] in the manner & time specified as above, and paying my debts, & defraying the charge of my funeral, and taking the care and charge of the maintenance & education of my children....

---

3. Edwards had specified what each of his children was to receive from his estate.

SELECT BIBLIOGRAPHY

In the past forty years the books, essays, and doctoral theses on Jonathan Edwards' theology have become a veritable flood. Yet there still remains much to be done regarding various details of his piety. For example, there still needs to be written a major study of Edwards' theology of prayer.[1] Now, central to any study of Edwards' piety are his many works—sermons, essays, and notebooks—that are currently being published in the Yale University Press edition of *The Works of Jonathan Edwards.* Hopefully, the letters in this selection will spur the reader on to reading and absorbing the riches in the rest of Edwards' corpus.

Those interested in digging deeper into the writings of Edwards should consult Joel R. Beeke and Randall J. Pederson, *Meet the Puritans: With a Guide to Modern Reprints* (Grand Rapids: Reformation Heritage Books, 2006), 193-233. Following a brief biographical sketch of Edwards, the authors present an annotated bibliography of Edwards' books reprinted between 1956 and 2005.

For a superb, comprehensive essay on Edwards' piety, see Charles Hambrick-Stowe's "The 'Inward, Sweet Sense' of Christ in Jonathan Edwards" in D.G.

---

1. Peter Beck, a Ph.D. student at Southern Baptist Theological Seminary, is currently engaged in doing his dissertation on this area of Edwards' life and thought.

Hart, Sean Michael Lucas, and Stephen J. Nichols, eds., *The Legacy of Jonathan Edwards: American Religion and the Evangelical Tradition* (Grand Rapids, Michigan: Baker, 2003), 79-95. For the pneumatological foundations of Edwards' piety, see the excellent study by Robert W. Caldwell III, *Communion in the Spirit: The Holy Spirit as the Bond of Union in the Theology of Jonathan Edwards* (Bletchley, Milton Keynes/Waynesboro, Georgia: Paternoster, 2006).

Probably the one work of Edwards that provides the best vista on his spirituality is his A Treatise Concerning Religious Affections (1746), which can be found in *The Works of Jonathan Edwards*, vol. 2. Its classic quality was soon recognized. For instance, before the end of the eighteenth century the Baptist educator and author John Ryland, Jr. (1753-1825), told a fellow Baptist pastor, Joseph Kinghorn (1766-1832), that if he could keep but three books out of his whole library, Edwards' *Religious Affections* would be one of the three.[2] For some recent discussions of this work, see Iain D. Campbell, "Jonathan Edwards' Religious Affections as a Paradigm for Evangelical Spirituality," *Scottish Bulletin of Evangelical Theology,* 21 (2003): 166-186; Mark R. Talbot, "Godly Emotions (Religious Affections)" in John Piper and Justin Taylor, eds., *A God Entranced Vision of All Things: The Legacy of Jonathan Edwards* (Wheaton, Illinois: Crossway Books, 2004), 221-256; and Stephen R. Holmes, "Religious Affections by Jonathan Edwards

---

2. Cited in Martin Hood Wilkin, *Joseph Kinghorn, of Norwich: A Memoir* (1855 ed.; repr. in *The Life and Works of Joseph Kinghorn* [Springfield, Missouri: Particular Baptist Press, 1995], I, 183).